WESTERN
COLORADO
FRUIT & WINE

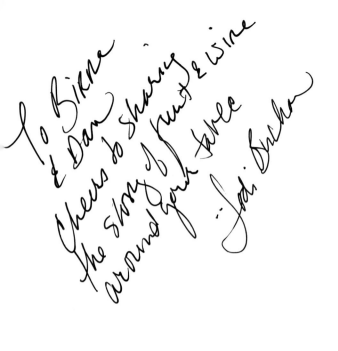

To Bienie
& Dan
Cheers to sharing
the story of fruit & wine
around your table

Jodi Buchan

JODI BUCHAN

WESTERN COLORADO FRUIT & WINE

A BOUNTIFUL HISTORY

AMERICAN PALATE

Published by American Palate
A Division of The History Press
Charleston, SC 29403
www.historypress.net

Front cover: Grapes hanging on vine; a Palisade peach ripening on the vine
in August; bee in sunflower; autumn vineyard rows at Canyon Wind Cellars
on byway. *Author photos.*
Back cover: High Country Orchards has nine thousand cherry trees. Cherries are among the
first fruit harvested in the Colorado crop calendar. *Courtesy High Country Orchards & Vineyards.*
Western Slope seasonal markets like Mt. Garfield Fruit and Vegetable Stand in Clifton
overflow with freshness during harvest season; Terror Creek Winery vineyards in the North
Fork Valley. *Author photos.*

First published 2015

Manufactured in the United States

ISBN 978.1.62619.780.0

Library of Congress Control Number: 2015938640

Notice: The information in this book is true and complete to the best of our knowledge. It is
offered without guarantee on the part of the author or The History Press. The author and
The History Press disclaim all liability in connection with the use of this book.

This book is dedicated to my brave ancestors, the Lucys, who homesteaded in the high, windy prairie of the Rendezvous Region in northeast North Dakota.

CONTENTS

ACKNOWLEDGEMENTS

People are stories. I heard that along this journey. Fruit and wine have a story thanks to those early explorers and historians whose ink has long since dried…and thanks to the archivists who preserved their words, providing a trail from the present into the past. I am greatly indebted to them, especially the local historians.

Hotchkiss-Crawford Historical Museum director Kathy McKee and volunteer Marilyn Bruce Tate searched, copied and scanned their museum and personal files to share with me collections of labels and photos, as well as their personal genealogies that trace back to some of the North Fork Valley's first settlers. Palisade Historical Museum chair Priscilla Bowman Walker in the Grand Valley was nothing short of a walking library of information—an encyclopedia of local lore—born of her family's history in the fruit industry's first days. Her passion for preservation was infectious and her desire to tell Palisade's story evident in her compilation of videos and books. Kay Fiegel and Anamae Richmond escorted me into a living history of fruit at the Museum of Western Colorado's Cross Orchards Historical Site.

All across the Western Slope, people I spoke with entrusted me with the story of their work in organizations that support the fruit-farming culture, their personal lives and those in their family trees. They shared anecdotes of struggles and passion and matter-of-fact farming. They opened their doors to reveal the "who" behind Colorado fruit and wine, sometimes around a meal at the dining table, as was the case with Harry and Bonnie Talbott. Thanks to those of you, too, whose histories are intricate parts of the tale but whose voices are not heard in the book.

Rick Turley (Colorado Cellars) gave me my first lesson on Western Slope wine history early in the process, and Doug Caskey, among others, including Jay Christianson (Canyon Wind Cellars) and Glenn Foster (Talon Wine Brands), continued the education. Many thanks to Western Colorado Research Center's viticulturist extraordinaire Horst Caspari for his insights and background on the Four Corners experiment.

Along the way, I had the pleasure of some traveling companions: Diana Saenz, who came to the Lavender Festival with me, enduring temperatures in the upper nineties in Grand Junction (thank goodness for the parasols they loaned us at Sage Creations Organic Farm during our tour); Juli Foy, who came with me to the Peach Festival, providing me with extra hands to juggle cameras and notepads as well as sisterly company; photographer Casey Hess, who accompanied me to Colorado Mountain Winefest, extending the reach of one person's lens to capture many beautiful photographs that I'd never have taken.

Of course, without the cooperation of the Colorado Association for Viticulture and Enology (CAVE) and Tour de Vineyards, who allowed me event access to take photographs, there would be fewer visual stories to enrich the text. Their coordinators—Cassidee Shull and Mike Heaston—and their staff went above and beyond to help Casey and me capture the moment.

The Isaacson School for New Media teachers and professors have been my storytelling mentors: Michael Conniff cracked my interview shell, Klaus Kocher focused my photographer's eye and *Aspen Sojourner* editor-in-chief Michael Miracle introduced me to the behind-the-scenes publishing world during my internship and guided me through word choice. It is one thing to put down a narrative, however, and quite another to get it to make sense as a whole. Kat Riseman looked at the first drafts—no easy task—and put her editorial skills to work. Her guidance and advice kept me moving forward and is the reason I didn't fall into writer's no man's land. Melissa Monahan Jankovsky took her proofing pen to the pages and saved me from many embarrassing missteps. Any remaining errors are clearly my own. Then there are The History Press editors Artie Crisp and Elizabeth Farry. As my project coordinator, Crisp exhibited great organizational feats in his oversight, and Farry waved her magic pen over the manuscript with great care.

In all of this indebtedness, there is artist and lifelong friend Vicky Moore Jacobs, without whom there would have been no idea for the book. I'd still be sipping wine and grilling peaches without knowing their Western Slope history, a knowledge that makes them all the more flavorful. Your creative and philanthropic energy never ceases to astound me.

And thank you to my husband, Glenn, who dances with me in the kitchen.

INTRODUCTION

We must give standing to the new pioneers…devoted to the building of agriculture and culture to match the scenery presented to those first European eyes.
—*Wes Jackson,* Becoming Native to This Place, *1992*

What you see when you enter the Grand and North Fork Valleys is a land tamed by persevering pioneers. Paved and dirt county roads lead to their fields, where today descendants and newcomers put on their boots to preserve the hardworking tradition of raising fruit. Western Slope orchards and vineyards are gateways to the past where passersby pull over, anticipating the first of the season's cherries or apricots or heirloom tomatoes—a favorite crop grown by the North Fork's late, great Joe Cocker. They sample jams and salsas, nibble on slices of crisp apples, sip on uncorked blends or Gewurztraminer and catch the scent of roasting peppers. They stop to smell the lavender. It is an unpretentious landscape, slowed to a tractor's pace while the world beyond its borders rushes by from neon stoplight to left-hand turn lane with coffee in the cup holder, french fries between the seats, takeout, dine in, "to go." Heaps of produce and packaged bounty ride grocery store treadmills, past the checker and into bags for the trek back through the green, yellow, red and the right-hand turn lane to the street sign home.

Home to those who live and farm on the Western Slope is a place where farm-to-table fare like Elk Osso Buco is partnered with wines from valley vintners like Stone Cottage Cellars, espresso is served in a historic apple shed and artisan showcases like the Blue Pig Gallery are community centers of creativity. It is a place where the proprietor is often the one in the tasting room pouring your wine or slicing up a fresh Glohaven—unless it is harvest season and they are still out in the orchard climbing up and down the ladder picking peaches. More than anything, though, the Western Slope is a place of stories passed on and shared.

With pen and paper, the aid of a tape recorder and an air-conditioned vehicle, I traveled to the tales. I visited museums where caretakers of local history opened the archive doors for me. I learned from humble experts about microclimates, ecosystems and beneficial bugs. I listened while a viticulturist told me how vines are individuals and each plant deserves attention. From farm to farm, historian to horticulturist—regardless of acreage, individual philosophies, age or gender—they have a commonality that ties them together: their lives are connected to the land, and they are connected to each other because of this.

Neighbor Gail reports that she has spent countless hours canning peach/ jalapeno salsa, tomatoes, applesauce and more. I went over and had a sample of those treats and man oh man. Yummmm! So far I've bagged and frozen nectarines and peaches. Next, the apples! Can't wait to make fall and winter's cold night suppers complete with a bowl of cinnamon applesauce. This month I will prepare the best soups ever and have them ready for company by the fire.
—Marla Bear Bishop, North Fork Merchant Herald*: "Up Front: The Bearattitudes, the Blessing of the Animals, Canning and Fall," 2014*

THE LAND THAT PEACHES BUILT

We see, through the mists of the present, the fruit-lands of the future.
—*William E. Pabor,* Fruit Culture in Colorado, *1883*

When visionary explorers breached the mountainous "back-bone of the continent" in Colorado, they looked to the western valleys, seeing beyond the rocky cliffs, the sagebrush and isolated expanses. Early settlers of the North Fork Valley Samuel Wade, George Duke and Enos Hotchkiss discovered wild gardens of thorn apple and berries that hinted at a fruitful region. Author and agriculturist William E. Pabor envisaged a watershed of growth for the Grand Valley, reminiscent of that in Kansas and Missouri.[1] Before their eyes was no American fruited plain nor was it a mirage. In their imagining, they saw a future landscape—one with possibility, prosperity and peaches.

Dreams of the ambitious booster or pioneering farmer were inspirations, seedlings of an idea that required a place to grow, but none could start a new story in a new land unless the land conceded a beginning.

NOT A MIRAGE

Colorado's Western Slope is sculpted with valleys that begin on the spine of the Rocky Mountains' Continental Divide—the imaginary line that splits the continent and is a high point in Colorado that directs water's natural flow either east or west. Streams that begin with snow and swell with melt and rain carve through the terrain, joining like veins to an artery, coursing downward until they reach wider, gentler gradients. The sun shines an average of 300 days annually. Although Western Slope precipitation is more consistent than on Colorado's Eastern Slope, the semiarid western valleys receive only seven to fourteen inches of precipitation a year in contrast to Peach County, Georgia's forty-four annual inches.[2] Wind coming out of the DeBeque Canyon into Palisade and airstreams channeling in at the head of the North Fork Valley near Paonia is dubbed by locals as the "million dollar breeze" and helps to protect vulnerable spring blossoms from frost. The sum result is an average 160–190 growing days that fill a crop calendar from May to November and, with irrigation resources, near-ideal fruit-growing conditions—if irrigation is available.

In the late 1800s, however, the Western Colorado region was dry and undeveloped. It was not public domain and was also part of the ever-shrinking Ute Indian territory. This was a factor that delayed rather than deterred exploration. So after yet another treaty transplanted the Utes in 1880 and the last of their bands were escorted out at the sound of an army bugle,[3] a modest number of enterprising settlers moved in. Published geological surveys that documented the value of western land did little to entice the general public east of the Continental Divide. The Western Slope remained a *terra incognita*, thanks in part to the lack of infrastructure but even more so due to the negative press images and reports.

An 1880 *Denver Tribune* article reported that, with little exception, Western Slope land is "about as valuable as…the Desert of the Sahara." In 1888, the United States Department of Agriculture "declared Colorado unfit for fruit production."[4] And in a Grand Valley circular written by area promoters meant to draw new populations, the authors, while stating the productivity potential, simultaneously presented a cautionary invite:

> *The soil has a dull grayish appearance, with hardly a blade of grass growing in it for several miles back from the river, and it produces naturally only sagebrush and greasewood. It is uninviting and desolate looking in the extreme…We are thus explicit in speaking of the desolate appearance of the country, so that no homesick wanderer in this far-off western land will say when his heart fails him in looking over our valley, that he has been deceived…If the reader of this lives in the east, he will almost surely be disappointed at first, if he comes out here.[5]*

"Waiting for water—residence of H.B. Tyler in NW1/4 of sect.21, T95, R103W—August 21, 1913." *Photo courtesy Grand Valley Water Users' Association, Grand Junction, CO.*

The ambitious groups that did stake out the West eventually proved the pessimistic optimist authors correct in their conclusion that even though the land does not make a good first impression, "it is one of the most productive valleys in Colorado." The voice that spoke the loudest on its behalf was the quality of the fruit.

In 2010, Colorado had 2,400 acres of peach orchards, which produced 14,000 tons of peaches (12,000 were utilized). The average peach yield per bearing acre between 2001 and 2010 was 5.7 tons.[6]

FRUIT'S FAMILY TREE

The root of the tree began with the pioneers. Following the discovery of thriving native fruit growth in the valleys fed by the North Fork of the Gunnison and its tributaries by Wade, Hotchkiss and their traveling companions in 1881, Wade returned the following year. He brought with him an "experimental bill" of trees, plants and varieties from Missouri, including two hundred apple trees, two hundred cherry trees, one hundred grape vines, along with various berries and a small sampling

Looking like sandstone books on a shelf, the rocky Book Cliffs range extends two hundred miles from the DeBeque Canyon in Colorado to Utah's Price Canyon. *Author photo.*

of peaches (twenty), apricots and pears. Wade's plantings, the first in the area, proved after some trial and error that North Fork's trilogy of geological factors—soil, climate and availability of streams that fed the Gunnison River—were fruit favorable.[7]

During this same time, George Crawford and a group of men selected the site for Grand Junction Town Company in the Grand Valley. Albeit an inconvenient 150 miles from the nearest railroad, the location was at the confluence of two major water sources: the Gunnison and Colorado (named Grand at the time) Rivers.[8] Irrigation projects began almost immediately. Early settlers Blain, Steele and Harlow all set up apple and peach orchards lined with saplings in the eastern end of the valley and Rapid Creek, a couple of miles out of Palisade.[9] Approximately three years later, the peach trees matured and bore the first fruit of the valley.

During this early activity, Eastern Slope journalist and fruit-farming advocate William E. Pabor published his twelve-year study, *Colorado as an Agricultural State: Its Farms, Fields, and Garden Lands*, and his book of compiled horticultural expertise, *Fruit Culture in Colorado: A Manual of Information*, in 1883. Pabor was so passionate about the Grand Valley's potential in particular that he bought barren land several miles west of Grand Junction,

where he planted trees and vines. There he founded the town of Fruitvale (now Fruita), the valley's "first fruit-tract community."[10]

Fruit was but a fledgling industry in the West—mining still maintained the nucleus of activity and economy. Fortunately for Western Slope growers, the mountain region miner camps and towns provided the necessary stimulus for a new industry: a locavore market. Pabor observed in *Colorado as an Agricultural State*:

> *The miners pay cash. The harvest gathered from the soil, under the genial influence of the sun and water, is as golden as that taken from the hills, whose supposed wealth attracts so many prospectors…The mines furnish a very profitable market, and towns are springing up in every direction.*

Pabor added that food imported from California, Utah, Kansas and Nebraska "ought to be raised at home."

So it was. Only nine years after the initial plantings, Delta County had 600 acres of producing orchards and Mesa County an approximated 1,500 acres, with some trees yielding one hundred pounds each.[11] Throughout that time, the public tasted for themselves the fruits of the region. Farther east, the fruit began to garner awards: North Fork growers, including Wade, won six first-place prizes for their entries at the 1893 Chicago World's

Fair.[12] Fruit farms sprouted up from Mesa County to Montezuma County to McElmo Canyon in Southwestern Colorado—the home of the winning peaches at the 1904 Saint Louis World's Fair.[13] And at the National Apple Exposition of 1910 in Denver, Grand Junction's carload of apples won the "grand sweepstakes."

The word was out. Fruit from the Western Slope was not only high in quality, but it was also a promising cash crop for those who wanted to build a life out west. A ready supply of irrigation water streamed through the mesas and lowlands. Land was plentiful and cheap...early on. Some property was available through the 1860s Homestead Act, a law signed by President Lincoln that granted land "free and clear" to claimants after five years of "residency" and "cultivation."[14] Other obtainable land came out of a preemptive from the Ute Reservation bill that enabled settlers to purchase "up to 160 acres" from the U.S. General Land Office at $1.25 per acre.[15] The primary resource this isolated region of Colorado lacked was people.

Land developers and community promoters peddled the Western Slope to seasoned East and Midwest farmers, as well as any new home-seeking greenhorns who would buy in. Grand Junction boosters called the valley "Little Empire of the Western Slope."[16] Newspaper editors and journalists, chambers of commerce and land developers' claims, community events and festivals,[17] along with railroad propaganda were all a siren's song intended to lure immigrants to the Western Slope.[18]

People from Maine to the Midwest to the Colorado mine boom-gone-bust communities responded.

Clark Family Orchards' ancestor James A. Clark heard about the "empire" while driving cattle on the Oregon Trail. He went back to his home in Iowa, packed up his family and moved to Palisade, coming by emigrant train car and planting their first trees in 1897.[19] New settlers came from other states like Kansas and Missouri, as well as Iowa. In fact, so many emigrated from Iowa that in 1907 Grand Junction established an annual "Iowa Day." During that era, the valley had twice as many Iowa transplants as any other state.[20]

Individual families and trainloads of people—sometimes fifty in one group—moved into the Palisade area.[21] In addition to the families looking for new agricultural opportunities, investors caught the fruit fever. Financiers and absentee owners invested in fruit ranches. Massachusetts investors Walter and Isabelle Cross funded one of the largest in the state. Their Red Cross Land and Fruit Company purchased 243 acres near Grand Junction and planted twenty-two thousand trees.[22]

Fruit farming gained popularity. Speculating "sharks" capitalized on this and drove land values up. The 1910 State Horticulture Board's annual report cautioned the "eastern homeseeker" against unreasonable expectations.[23] Still, the Grand Valley enjoyed an agricultural momentum. Other cash crops, including sugar beets during the Spanish-American War, even had a run of popularity.[24]

By the late 1800s and early 1900s, the apple became king under the Mount Garfield crown in the Grand Valley, followed by pear and peach in terms of economic royalty.[25] The apple boom had worms, however—one literal, one figurative and one concocted.

In 1905, Spencer Seedless Apple Company sent four of their anomalies—a seedless variety—to a European crowned head. His Majesty King Edward of

The 2014 Peach Festival's crowned winner from "Harry's Peaches" is a Glohaven weighing in at one pound, fifteen ounces. *Author photo.*

England uttered a diplomatic proclamation: "Delicious; the best apple I have ever tasted." The royal endorsement was flattering but did not help Spencer's ill-fated attempt to rid the apple of its seeded center or secure Spencer its desired investors. The apples, harvested from a rumored single producing tree, had no flavor and poor quality. The scheme rotted into obscurity shortly (a reported nine days) after its initial announcement.[26]

The factor that ate away at apple yields, however, wasn't in the core. It was at the roots. Seepage due to unlined dirt furrows with no run-off avenues saturated the plants. Without run-off channels, the roots drowned in excess water. The literal larva was the codling moth. To combat the grubby invader, orchardists wrapped the trunks with fabric[27] and took to the fields with lead arsenate spray—poisons ingested by the insect.[28] This left the industry with a double-edged dilemma: poison had to be washed off the apples before they could be shipped, but washing the fruit degraded its integrity.[29]

Weakened by these adverse methods and pests, as well as a killing freeze in May 1915 that destroyed many apple crops, the valley crowned a new economic monarch. The peach became queen and has ruled ever since, in spite of many attempts by weather, pests, downturns and development.

Ripe for the Pickin'

The 1930s brought in hard times for the peach industry. Fruit values had already been on a decline following the inflated WWI prices. Then across the state, the Great Depression shut down mining operations, logging mills and pocket books of consumers in statewide and national markets.[30]

Steadfast farmer owners had a resource that city dwellers didn't during the crisis: land…and water. The earth they tended aided their survival. Their wares were edible—if not sparsely spread on the table during the '30s—providing a basic need rather than that of paper money and minerals. They could live off what the earth provided, not what the metro soup kitchens ladled out. Fifth generation Palisade peach grower Dennis Clark says of his ancestors: "They had their own meat, dairy, chickens—they had the ground."[31] Irrigated land was a life-sustaining soil for those dedicated to working the earth for their livelihood.

The stimulus that followed the days of hardships came in the form of WWII in the 1940s. Delta, Montrose and Montezuma Counties supplied over one-fifth of Colorado's peach harvest, increasing to 28.2 percent by

1945. The dollar value from 1940 to 1950 "increased by over $1,250,000."[32] Peach production was growing, and so was the Grand Valley, the regional nucleus for cycles of energy booms and bursts sparked now by uranium and oil shale.[33]

As the eighties rolled forward, so did the bulldozers. Orchards were flattened. Housing developments replaced the rows of fruit trees.[34] At the eleventh hour, 24 acres of peach giant Red Cross Land and Fruit Company's 243 acres were saved, eventually becoming Museum of Western Colorado's living farm, Cross Orchards Historical Site. Site director Kay Fiegel retells the story:

> *There were trees as tall as buildings. The place was just about to be demolished—they had a wrecking machine here. A nurse from St. Mary's Hospital called the Museum of Western Colorado and said, "you've got to do something. They're going to destroy the Cross Barn." The community just pounced on it. Bray Real Estate Company matched property, the Friends of the Museum held a raffle, and clubs like Territorial Daughters and 4-H joined in.*

The increase in population caused conflicts between the developing suburbia and the orchardists, such as the Ela family, who came to the Grand

Members of the Western Colorado Chapter of the Territorial Daughters of Colorado were key volunteers in the refurbishing of Cross Orchards Historical Site's bunkhouse pictured here. *Author photo.*

Cross Orchards Historical Site provides a living history experience in Grand Junction. *Author photo.*

Junction area from Iowa in 1909. They began farming fruit in 1920 and continued there into the mid-'90s, until development pressures "were getting more extreme." Urbanization was melding into the pastoral corridors, and the two cultures didn't always coincide harmoniously.[35]

Steve Ela, owner of Ela Family Farms, recalls, "There was one night one of our guys was spraying—we spray at night because that's when the wind is calm—and my uncle got a call, 'Get that *bleep, bleep, bleep* guy off the sprayer or I'll shoot him off.'" He says the threat probably wouldn't have been carried out, but there was other vandalism: trees cut down and irrigation system sets where people had pulled the dams. "Nothing huge," says Ela, adding, "On the whole neighbors were great, but there's always a couple people…It only takes one." Ela's family moved their operations near Hotchkiss in 1995, following the lead of his uncle, who had already planted new roots in the North Fork Valley.

THE CORE OF NORTH FORK VALLEY

A souvenir publication from Paonia's *The Newspaper* just after the turn of the twentieth century defined the North Fork Valley in words that can still be used in 2014: "desirable" community of "thrift and intelligence," composed of "self-made-men" and people of "public spirit."[36] That early

North Fork peaches heading to the Colorado State Fair in 1909. *Photo courtesy Hotchkiss-Crawford Historical Society.*

pioneering spirit also extended into the future, to the new settlers in the North Fork—only today, instead of terrain, it is technology with fruit the common denominator linking the past to the present.

Fruit has been the shining star in the North Fork of Delta County; fruit farming was the townships' founding economic catalyst. It helped to create a culture of orchardists who established themselves as citizens of note: Samuel Wade, Paonia merchant and postmaster; J.A. Rovaart, bank "director"; state representative Honorable C.M. Hammond; justice of the peace Judge Wm. B. Osboldstone; and Enos Hotchkiss (Hotchkiss town founder), who declined all but one prompting—county commissioner—to enter into the civic limelight.

A newspaper article from 1909 reported with undertones of civic pride the events of the Colorado State Fair in Pueblo. In a "monstrous undertaking," Delta County community members loaded a train car with peaches, sent it to Pueblo and handed out a free peach to fair goers "just as fast as the people could walk up and get it." At the end of the exhibition, the fruit was not sold off. Rather, in the spirit of community that echoes through the present-day North Fork Valley, they gave it to a local orphanage. Delta County growers went home with twenty first-place recognitions, including "plate of peaches of any variety," "best plate pears" and several apple variety winners in addition to the "much-desired" Jonathan. In spite of this notoriety, fruit was not the only winning entry.[37] The North Fork community also received "best art exhibit from public schools"—a connection of art and agriculture from yesteryear that contributed to a current artistic valley culture and to their attained Certified Creative District status in 2013.[38]

North Fork growers branched off the introductory success of World Fair wins to become the "It" place in the state for fruit in the new decade of the twentieth century. The award-winning fruit, along with area boosters, garnered its reputation in the 1920s as "the Core of Apple Country."[39] Delta County greeted that decade as the top producer in Colorado for apple and apricot trees.[40] They got through the fruit shortages and economic difficulties of the '30s and entered into the '40s and '50s on a barrel roll of prosperity, contributing to the Western Slope's escalating peach values and apple production.[41]

As the century advanced, the isolated North Fork Valley was not completely immune to the pressures of western development, mining and rising land costs. Continuing into the new millennium, still without an epicenter like Grand Junction and with 55 percent of the lands designated public use, Delta County, and the North Fork Valley in particular, lent itself to small-scale farming and innovation. Market competition and a pioneering ethos have put Delta County in Colorado's forefront of biodynamic, organic and natural farming practices: the tangy-sweet juice pressed from an apple that is the result of restraint and stewardship is nothing short of "delicious."

Flavorful Festivals

The Palisade Peach Festival began in Grand Junction as a county fair theme. County fairs have been a midway of Mesa County agriculture awareness since the late nineteenth century. Early fair exhibitions included "Kitchen and Pantry Stores," "Fine Arts" and "Farm Animals," in addition to fruit and vegetables. The local druggist set up toiletries to catch the interest of passersby, and other displays included M. Strous's merchant wares: bear hides, beaver skins, overcoats, moccasins and gloves. Organizers infused new and expanded energy into the annual event in 1891, adding baseball, horse races, a rodeo and a "Fireman's Tournament" with a parade and competitions between Colorado volunteer fire departments from Aspen to Durango. They aligned the fair with the harvest and branded the event "Peach Day." With the escalating economic importance of peaches, led by the Elberta, fruit became the spotlight speaker for the region.

President Taft stopped by the event when he swung through Grand Junction in 1909. A record ten thousand people attended the fair that day, hoping to get a glimpse, share community needs—especially with respect to irrigation support from the government—and hear his views of the Western Slope. The president was a grandstand hit among attendees with diplomatic statements like how they were a community of "an independence of thought with a quickness of perception that indicates a rapidly progressing people" and how the area was "one of the important parts of the United States." Irrigation funding for the High Line Canal followed diplomacy. The appropriation was aided perhaps by Taft's train trip to Western Colorado through what he observed as "the most God-forsaken spot…on earth" into the irrigated Grand Valley, where the transformed terrain "seems like a paradise."[42]

The president's visit was the pinnacle of Peach Days. The fair began to lose money. Other festivities competed for the public: "Iowa Day," a celebration that began in 1907 in honor of the many Iowan transplants, and the Fruit Belt Route festivities in Fruita starting in 1910.[43] Peach Days ceased altogether in 1923. The Fair Association sold the grounds—now Lincoln Park—to the city of Grand Junction.

A festival promoting peaches lay dormant in the Grand Valley until the late 1960s, when the Palisade Chamber of Commerce created a Palisade Peach Festival. A sponsorship, community and civic collaboration, the festival has become a major agritourism draw and chamber fundraiser. "It's a destination event," Palisade Chamber of Commerce executive director Juliann Adams says. "The Peach Festival has become an annual shopping trip—even of wine—for many people."

At the forty-sixth annual celebration in August 2014, over fifteen thousand fruit fans joined in festivities at Riverbend Park, the host location since 2003. Peach juice ran off cutting boards as vendors handed out slices of their bounty. An Ice-Cream Social & Dance event, along with music, carriage rides and kids' games contributed to the atmosphere of the chamber's motto, "Life Tastes Good Here." Guided historical walking tours, self-guided tours to farms and vineyards along the county roads and agri-tours hosted by orchardists expanded the geography beyond park perimeters. Feast in the Field offered a more recent tradition for those with a culinary inclination. Revolving hosts, including Z's and Suncrest Orchards in 2014, provided the setting for a four-course gourmet dinner prepared by local restaurant chefs and served with Colorado wine on tables set up for diners in the orchards.

Farm fare, youth and community take center stage in Paonia with the Mountain Harvest Festival in September. Mountain Harvest Festival is

Peach Festival booths offer try-before-you-buy tastes from farms like Palisade's Juicy Acres. *Author photo.*

both an annual event and a public charity organization. As a nonprofit organization, it provides youth scholarships, literacy programs and general education opportunities; collaborates with other philanthropic community ventures; and supports "agriculture and food sciences." The fourteen-year-old event is music and market, performance art and agriculture. Mountain

Harvest Festival director Heidi Hudek writes about the happening in her event guide message:

> *In this copious valley we are blessed with a plethora of fine crops, a community of generous and fervent people, and an abundant array of talent; all surrounded by a rich beauty which reminds us to take pause and be at peace…Mountain Harvest Festival is a celebration of our bounty. Harvest time lends a feeling of prosperity, benevolence, and indulgence.*

Produce-specific festivals highlight the agricultural diversity in both valleys and are often scheduled when those crops—or their activities—are at their peak. One of the older festivals is North Fork Valley Cherry Days on the Fourth of July. The Paonia Lions Club devised it in 1947 for the purpose of raising money for football field lights. It has remained a community cornerstone ever since. More recent fêtes include the Lavender Festival later in July, which highlights the floral wonders in both valleys, and the April Palisade International Honey Bee Festival. The bee festival was founded by local beekeeper Tina Darrah with the intent of raising awareness "in support of a healthy honey bee population worldwide and its impact on agriculture and society."

Western Slope fruit culture has matured beyond crop yields, influencing activities and economic growth beyond the orchard rows. Festivals have transitioned past community pride and development into vacation destinations. Farms are no longer a place to grow things—they are the sites of public education, events and even lodging. Agritourism has become an American pastime and a dollar-driver for rural areas. The Colorado Department of Agriculture reported in the USDA 2012 Ag Census, "864 Colorado farms offered agritourism and recreational services, totaling nearly $30 million in farm income."[44]

Agritourism is the new frontier, the modern face of diversification for Western Slope farmers.

27

2

THROUGH THE GRAPE (AND) VINE

I confess that I am just a little bit "nutty" on the subject of foreign grapes but the distemper has been on the increase since I began to know just a little bit about this marvelous product—the vine. If I were to see some of the bottles of wine made away back in the middle ages I should certainly want to break the total abstinence pledge and take a "wee bit of a drop."
—Honorable A.C. Newton,
Annual Report of the State Board of Agriculture, *1910*[45]

The Western Slope wine industry was born of a passion for the grape—first by early immigrants whose culture it was to serve wine with the daily bread and later with a few key home hobby winemakers. The hobbyists ended up making more than wine. They made a wine country. Those kitchen-table alchemists took risks, educated themselves and siphoned resources from California and Oregon. The names of the initial winery entrepreneurs might not be commonly known to many vino enthusiasts, but they are Colorado wine history pioneers: Jim and Ann Seawald, who co-founded Western Colorado's first winery, Colorado Mountain Vineyards (now Colorado Cellars); Mary and Parker Carlson from Carlson Vineyards; and DeBeque Canyon Winery's ubiquitous Bennett Price.

The land, too, has played its part. Terroir features like geography, climate and boundaries define Western Colorado's only American Viticultural Areas (AVAs), Grand Valley and West Elks, and influence the wine's characteristics and complexities. (Napa and Sonoma Valleys in California, for example, are

Winefest "hands-free" wine glass holders. *Photo by Casey Hess.*

AVAs.) Ultimately, the climates and microclimates trained the growth of the Western Slope wine industry, pruning out the weak varieties with winterkill and spring frosts and revealing slowly over time and education the vines, viticulture and enology that embody a region's identity.

This aging, maturing of effort and region, has produced a unique wine country—one that, against all odds and humble beginnings, has produced award-winning vintages and become an acclaimed taster's destination.

APPELLATION OF ORIGIN

The history of winemaking on the Western Slope starts with a raised glass and a toast to the Europeans who settled in the West.

When Europeans traveled to the New World to work in the mines, on the railroads and as stonemasons, they came with their Old World tradition of winemaking. Wine has long been a mealtime staple of many European cultures.[46] So when Italians, Austrians, Slovenians and the French settled in Colorado, it was only natural that they planted vines.

In the North Fork Valley's stepped terrain of plateaus and vistas, Frenchman Clement Fougnier bought Wade's Terror Creek orchard property on Garvin Mesa near the turn of the twentieth century. He planted viniferous grapes—grapes for wine—and gained a valley-wide reputation for his *vin* that drew visitors to his home when roads and transportation were arduous and there was no social media to spread the word.[47]

Over in the Grand Valley, Italian immigrants laid down their roots in geography reminiscent of their homelands.[48] Among the early home cellar

The Palisade Fruit & Wine Byway includes views of the Grand Mesa, the largest flattop mountain in the world. *Author photo.*

enologists were John Goffredi, Valentino Gobbo and Pete Landini. Enter, too, the Slovenians who also practiced enology for the friends and family table: First came miner and farmer Frank Marolt, as well as the Kladdocks and, nearly seventy years later, Denverite Gerald Ivancie, who founded Colorado's first winery.[49]

Joining the Europeans in viticulture were Western Slope boosters, pioneers and visionaries. Influential notable and the "Father of Grand Junction" George Crawford is also reported to have included grapes with his fruit production in the Rapid Creek area near Palisade.[50] And Fruita's founding father—the Grand Valley's biggest supporter of the fruit industry—William E. Pabor planted grapes in 1883 that included the Muscat and Flame Tokay, European table grape species that had been used in winemaking.[51]

The vines thrived in the semiarid desert aided by improving irrigation methods. USDA Census for Agriculture Colorado reports in 1909 showed 254,292 vines yielding over one million pounds of grapes from 1,034 farms.[52] On the Western Slope from Rapid Creek to the "Vinelands" near Palisade and out to Fruita, grapes for wine—in addition to juice and jelly—became established crops. Established, that is, until Prohibition, when fervent Coloradans ripped them out.

A Dry Finish

The path to Prohibition began long before winemaking in Colorado. An "Awakening" movement in 1830 by abolitionists to rid the country of "sins," with slaveholding the powering offence, was the fermenting catalyst. As the religious and political agendas shifted through the years,[53] the voices of churches and previously mute women lifted to right further wrongs: labor laws, prison reform and suffrage. But not all were united on these fronts. The common denominator, their proclaimed "evil" unifying Democrats with Republicans, feminists with industrialists, the Ku Klux Klan with the NAACP was alcohol.[54] These normally contrary factions came together under the heavy-handed lobbying thumb of the Anti-Saloon League, and leading the Colorado charge to eradicate the scapegoat for social ills was the Woman's Christian Temperance Union.[55]

The *Cyclopedia of Temperance, Prohibition and Public Morals* (yes, *Cyclopedia*) was one of many pro-prohibition publications published by the Methodist

Book Concern. They defined "true" temperance as "moderation in the use of everything good, abstinence for the use of everything bad."[56] Religious activists celebrated in the streets with prayer and blessings when Colorado embraced this philosophy and turned it into law.[57] The Local Option Law enabled communities to proclaim their districts "anti-saloon territory," where "the keeping and sale of intoxicating liquors is prohibited, except as provided in this act" regardless of a state's statutes on prohibition.[58] The Woman's Christian Temperance Union on the Western Slope rallied around the law and pressed for a society free of saloons. They were effective: Mesa County "went dry in 1909,"[59] long before Colorado's "Bone Dry" prohibition[60] law in 1918 that preceded the Eighteenth Amendment to the Constitution, aka the Volstead Act, in 1920. The only town that didn't go dry with the rest of the county was Fruita—it already was by virtue of its founding principles.[61]

Vitis vinifera—wine grapes—growing activities in Colorado lay dormant from the forces of Prohibition. It was an industry waiting for a phoenix rising.

Vintage Experiment

When Denverite dentist Gerald Ivancie began Colorado's commercial wine industry, he took "rinse and spit" out of his periodontal office and onto the aerating taste buds of wine-tasting sophisticates. Ivancie honored his Slovenian winemaking heritage and began crafting wine in his Front Range home for family and friends with grapes imported from three California AVAs: Napa, Mendocino and Sonoma.[62] The bottled result of his efforts, aided by his wife and nine children, was a palate-pleasing success. Prompted by enthusiastic oenophiles of his garage wine, Ivancie sought mentorship from the California wine country to help him launch his commercial venture in 1968: Ivancie Wines.[63] His hired guide in all things viniferous was none other than Vintner Hall of Famer Warren Winiarski—Robert Mondovi winemaker at the time and eventual founder of Stag's Leap Wine Cellars (not to be confused with Stags' Leap Winery).[64]

Over the next five years, the price of California grapes tripled.[65] Colorado's enologist pioneers, led by Ivancie, looked to the Grand Valley for in-state growing potential. They met with Palisade agriculture teacher Curtis

Carlson Vineyards is one of Colorado's wine pioneers. Mary and Parker Carlson planted grapes in the early 1980s and opened their own winery on East Orchard Mesa in 1988. *Author photo*.

Talley for local insight and connections. The timing was right. Talley and five other growers, including George Zimmerman, recognized the need for crop diversification due to a "decline of the peach industry," following damage from recent severe weather. The group of five bought into Ivancie's idea of planting grapes, entering into an exclusivity contract with Ivancie's winery,[66] with Ivancie offering financial incentives if they would plant vines.[67] The group committed a combined total of twenty or so acres on their properties in Palisade, East Orchard Mesa and Grand Junction.

Thus began one of two simultaneous—and somewhat separate— experiments in the early 1970s that uncorked the Western Slope wine industry. The Ivancie group planted the first viniferous vines in Mesa County, and the Four Corners Regional Commission conducted a study, *Grape and Wine Production in the Four Corners Region*, that provided research and recommendations for growers looking to diversify into the wine industry. The Four Corners Region consists of northeast Arizona, southwest Colorado, northwest New Mexico and southeast Utah, as their boundaries meet at a quadripoint.

The Ivancie group sourced vines through the well-connected Winiarski. The initial plants came from California growers improperly prepped for transport and shipped unprotected. By the time they reached the Grand Valley, growers found the roots "bone dry." The stock all died. A second 1973 planting lived. But by the next year, their motivator and mentor Gerald Ivancie had left Ivancie Wines—for reasons that were partly to do with clashing in-house market/sales philosophies and partly financial, due to an end product (marketable wine) that was still years from bottling and would still require purchase of costly California grapes to supplement Colorado's sparse crops.

"Grape vines take three years to produce fruit, five to produce a full crop," explains Colorado Cellars owner Rick Turley. "Wine takes time to make. There was no wine available for sale in any quantity until 1980."

So when Ivancie Wines went out of business in 1975, the growers were committed to a crop with no mentor, no buyers and no market. Fortunately for Western Slope vintners and enologists—the "cellar rats"—help was already around the corner.

Concurrently, Colorado State University (CSU) became recipient of two grants. The Four Corners Regional Commission, whose mission is long-range planning with an eye toward economics, and a Four Corners grant awarded Colorado State University funds that enabled them to build a research station on East Orchard Mesa. The objective of the

A "Wine Aroma Wheel" and a lineup of glasses with flavor profile clues at Winefest help participants learn about taste complexities. *Photo by Casey Hess.*

commission study was to examine the viability of grape growing in the four corner states. The study focused on evaluations of "adaptability of grape varieties," "wine produced" and the utilization of "findings to establish viticultural regions." In other words, find out which grapes grow best, what the wine is like and create an AVA. Much of this analysis focused on climate. Elevation and inland environments in Western Colorado are unlike the major wine producing states of California and Washington. Palisade's elevation is 4,800 feet above sea level. Paonia's in the North Fork Valley is 5,645 feet. Both are one thousand miles from an ocean and without the benefit of a weather-tempering body of water. Additionally, with the proximity to the Rocky Mountains, viticulture needed to be tailored to the climate and the varieties cold hardy. While the Western Slope's hot days and cool nights do help to stress the grape—a balance that intensifies flavor—the region is subject to freezes. In the early years, growers experienced losses of up to 75 percent.[68]

To provide mentorship, a newly formed Regional Grape Advisory Board brought in wine industry experts, especially those from Washington State and the University of Arizona. Commission researchers involved with the study worked with area growers, studying the early Ivancie plantings and establishing new experimental plantings. Federal funds from the grants infused the novice industry with much-needed aid and guidance. The Commission's subsequent 1980 *Grape and Wine Production in the Four Corners Region* technical report stated the following:

> *It seems clear that better ways must be found to utilize our resources so as to provide a better life for our citizens. In agriculture it would seem that the development of crops which utilize less water, provide greater employment and provide a higher economic return need to be found. Studies have indicated that grapes are such a crop.*[69]

Vitis vinifera species—Cabernet Sauvignon, Merlot, Pinot Noir and Riesling for example—are thin-skinned grapes high in acidity used around the world for winemaking.

The project was an infusion of momentum and marketing. New planting experiments also went beyond the initial Ivancie group locations of Grand Junction and Palisade. Fritz Gobbo, son of Grand Valley Italian vine pioneer Valentine Gobbo, planted in Fruita. Above Paonia the Four Corners project planted vines on land that is now Terror Creek Winery. As of 2014, some of the Four Corner study's original experimental vines were still in existence, including Paonia's Terror Creek Winery and Palisade's Colorado Cellars.

Act I, II and III

In addition to the study, mentorship, visionary hobbyists and gumption of the Ivancie group, subsequent laws in 1977, 1990 and 2009 also aided fledgling Colorado wine producers.

The Colorado Limited Winery Act of 1977 helped to open the doors for small producers by establishing lower tax rates and enabling onsite tastings, retail and wholesale. Small operations defined as a "limited winery" meant "any establishment manufacturing not more than one hundred thousand gallons…of vinous liquors annually," or about forty-two thousand cases.[70] That's below half, for example, of the ninety-seven thousand cases Oregon top-twenty producer Willamette Valley Vineyards bottled in 2012.[71]

Next, the Colorado Wine Industry Development Act of 1990 became a research, development and promotional resource for those in the business. A new Colorado Wine Industry Development Board (CWIDB), a cultivator of information and dissemination for Colorado vintners and enologists, was incorporated into the act. Part of the required information, achieved through research and experimental plantings, is "to develop maximum yields and quality." The CSU Western Colorado Research Center at Orchard Mesa in Grand Junction is the responsible steward of the task. The foundation for their research foundation was born of the Four Corners study and based on the work done by viticulturist Rick Hamman. It has been continued into 2015 by CSU viticulturist Professor Horst Caspari.

One of CSU's newer research ventures is their own winery. Rams Point Winery's stated purpose is enology education for students and interns interested in "winemaking" and "business practices." Rams Point Winery bottled its first wine in 2013 under House Bill 08-1359 Revised Statute 12-47-106, which enables them to produce wine for research and education.[72] The educational winery's distribution is limited, with its target market mostly CSU alumni.[73] With CSU spending fiscal and labor resources working on the research and development portion, CWIDB takes the lead on marketing and promotion obligations, incorporating additional earmarked activities such as agritourism.

An "alternating proprietorship" law in 2009 gave smaller-sized wineries the opportunity for collaboration and resource sharing. It enabled them to "operate at an alternating license" location, meaning a grower could use another operation's winemaking facility for their own wine. One of the first partnerships on the Western Slope to utilize the benefit of more than one wine proprietor using a single winemaking location was relative Grand Valley newcomer Colterris Wines of Palisade and Two Rivers Winery and Chateau proprietors in Grand Junction. Two Rivers had the brick and mortar facility, Colterris the grapes—the result was a 2008 Cabernet Sauvignon blend that catapulted owners Theresa and Scott High into the Colorado wine scene.

Colorado's Grand Cru

Western Colorado was still in isolation—not so much in geography any longer—but in the wine industry. Shortly after becoming the director of CWIDB and the official voice of Colorado wines, Doug Caskey related the challenge in a BizWest article: "Most Colorado consumers are still unaware that we even make wine in Colorado, let alone that we have won medals at the Los Angeles County Fair and many international competitions."

Meadery of the Rockies' bottles wear medals of bronze, silver and gold—including 2014 Class Champion at Houston Rodeo Uncorked!, an international wine competition with 2,500 entries. *Author photo.*

Rick Turley has been building his Colorado Cellars' wall of fame over the past twenty-five years. Cofounded by Jim Seawald as Colorado Mountain Vineyards in the late 1970s, it was the first winery on the Western Slope. *Author photo.*

Besides obscurity, Colorado wines had to overcome a public perception of poor quality. Talon Wine Brands owner Glenn Foster voices a common theme. "Originally Colorado wines were frowned upon," he says. "We've really gained a lot. The quality has been going up and up and up—perceptions have reflected that."[74]

National and worldwide competitions are one of the factors changing this perception.

Warren Winiarski was a judge in the 2014 Colorado Governor's Cup Winemaking Competition, a blind taste event—and he knows good wine. His Cabernet Sauvignon won the best red entry over French Bordeaux entries (Château Montrose, Château Haut-Brion and Château Mouton-Rothschild) in the 1976 Judgment of Paris tasting. "I was truly impressed with the quality and direction of Colorado's wine producers," Winiarski said in a CWIDB press release of the competition. "The industry has come a long way since I made wine here 46 years ago! Quite a number of the wines I tasted were beyond expressing merely the region but had the character of classics."[75]

The 2014 Governor's Cup winner Jay Christianson of Canyon Wind Cellars has experienced the journey from the past into present-day quality.

Christianson's geologist father, Norman, planted their first vines in 1991. Since taking over the winery from his parents in 1997, Christianson says he has learned "humbling lessons," including that the climate and the soil ultimately decide what to grow. He adds that along the way he's tried many grapes and made a few "poor decisions."

"Zinfandel is a perfect example—it just doesn't belong. This is not a hot climate for a long time. It is hot for a short time," says Christianson. "Tempernillo was a subjective bad decision. It didn't work for us. We pulled it out and put in Malbec."[76] At first, Christianson felt a sense of the property working against him. Over time, he discovered "a much more stewardship approach." Right now, Petit Verdot is getting his and the public's attention with his "Best Red Wine and Best of Show" win at the Governor's Cup, and the necks of their newer Anemoi label wines are draped in gold and silver medals.

Grape varietals have changed since the 1970s not only from trial-and-error plantings by CSU and growers like Christianson learning what thrives in Western Colorado but also from adapting to what consumers want. "White Zinfandel was a big thing twenty years ago," says Colorado Cellars' Rick Turley. He adds that it was Riesling and then Chardonnay in the '90s. Both Turley and Foster have expanded their offerings to reach an ever-broadening audience and palate. The Colorado wine consuming audience is definitely increasing.

The effort of public awareness beyond industry insiders by CWIDB and active growers like Canyon Wind Cellars, Colterris and others has expanded the customer base by leaps and vines. "The missing element of the locavore movement has always been Colorado wine," says Christianson, "and that's starting to change."

Over twenty years, the Colorado wine industry has sustained an above-average 16 percent growth rate. Economic impact numbers have tripled since 2005. Colorado wines keep racking up more regional, national and international awards.[77] And wine drinkers are coming to Western Colorado in record numbers for one of the most popular agritourism events in the state: Colorado Mountain Winefest.

Colorado Mountain Winefest held in September of each year in Palisade is a party with a purpose. It's the major fundraiser for the Colorado Association for Viticulture and Enology (CAVE). CAVE is a nonprofit advocate for the Colorado wine industry, founded originally as the Rocky Mountain Association of Vintners and Viticulturists in 1987 by a group of Western Slope growers, including those from Carlson, DeBeque and Plum Creek wineries. In 2010, it became CAVE, a 501(c)6 with a small staff of three. CAVE works with

Left: The Front Range's Boulder Creek Winery won Double-Gold in 2014 and a Warren Winiarski Special Commendation. *Photo by Casey Hess.*

Below: The Whitewater Hill Winery Fairy pours a 2012 vintage at Winefest. *Author photo.*

The Wine Country Inn hosts several events during Colorado Mountain Winefest, including the Chocolate & Wine Tasting with sweets from confectioners, including Enstrom's, a Grand Junction original. *Author photo*.

other associations throughout the state on networking, grower advocacy, marketing and raising public awareness through agritourism efforts such as the Palisade Fruit & Wine Byway. Part of their aim is to support up-and-coming winemakers through an amateur winemaking competition. Two of the winners have started wineries in the state.[78]

The first wine festival in 1992 was a grass-roots collaboration with the Grand Junction Visitor and Convention Bureau and the CWIDB. Held at Memorial Park in Palisade, volunteers ran the event, and five wineries participated. CAVE executive director Cassidee Shull says back then organizers were "begging and pleading people to come," with about five hundred people attending the first Colorado Mountain Winefest. By the 2014 Alpine Bank–sponsored twenty-third annual event, fifty-three wineries signed on, and over six thousand people from Utah, New Mexico, Texas, China, Australia, Germany, Poland and throughout Colorado ate, drank and learned about Colorado wines.

The festival takes place over four days and has evolved into a destination, community-wide event expanded by periphery activities such as Tour de Vineyards—an early morning cycle along the Palisade Fruit & Wine Byway. Highlights have included a winemakers' dinner and chocolate and wine tasting hosted by the Wine Country Inn; food and wine pairings at various restaurants in the Grand Valley; self-guided tours; a Plein Air wine, dine and paint; and the centerpiece at Palisade's Riverbend Park: Festival in the Park. The participants have "a good chance of being served by the owner at the wine tastings," Shull says, adding that the wineries are usually run by families and "very generational."

Colorado Mountain Winefest includes wineries from areas around the state that are not designated AVAs but are producing distinctly Colorado wines: McElmo Canyon and Montezuma County, South Grand Mesa, Olathe (sweet corn fame) and Montrose Counties in the west; and Fremont County and the Front Range in the east. Some enologists still use grapes from out of state to augment local variety and yields while others have committed to making Colorado wine with only Colorado-grown grapes, regardless of occasional production limitations. Imported, native or blended, wherever the grapes (or honey) come from, wine made in Colorado is a reflection of the region.

Viticulturists and enologists in the two Western Slope AVAs, Grand Valley and the West Elks, have had forty years to hone their skills, their knowledge maturing. The developing character of wine from Colorado's AVAs is what Doug Caskey describes as "an expression of place." It is a manifestation with

Paonia's Stone Cottage Cellars' owner Karen Helleckson describes their wines to festivalgoers. *Photo by Casey Hess.*

good legs in a stem glass. He adds, "[The profile is] tied to where it comes from—a connection between wine, land and people." Kyle Schlachter, CWIDB's outreach coordinator, summarizes the relationship between place and taste: "It's geography in a bottle."

3
ALL IN A DAY'S WORK

The peach dictates everything—seven days a week from dark to dark.
—*Steven Sherer, Aloha Organic Orchards, 2014*

Labor demands in Western Slope orchards begin in the late winter with the prune, before the sap runs and the buds break through. The work of shaping young trees and thinning crowded branches is methodical. When spring blossoms emerge, wind machines stand above the trees, sentinels at the ready to ward off potential killing frosts. The watch is twenty-four hours. Growers monitor orchard weather stations through the night, with bedside alarms in case they need to set the wind fans into motion to save the vulnerable crops. As summer nears, trees leaf out and fruit begins to form—they are the field workers. Then a steady flow of activities begins—fertilizing, weeding, pest control. When the fruit is full in color, juice and scent, it's all hands on harvest.

Fruit waits for no man, woman or child. When peaches, apples or pears are ripe, they need to be picked while in their prime to maintain the high standards of quality consumers expect. Harvest pace is urgent.

Small orchards of a few acres can be managed with a modest team of family members, neighbors and friends. Still, the work is no less intense—peach yields can average 5.7 tons per bearing acre—there are just fewer hands.[79] In the early years, regardless of the farm's size, the primary peach variety was the thin-skinned Elberta, and they ripened at the same time. Every able body helped pick, pack and ship during the brief two-week harvest.[80]

Sharing a harvest meal in the Talbotts' bunkhouse during WWII. *Photo courtesy Talbott Farms.*

With today's crop diversity in Western Colorado, picking season can begin in June and last until October, with some operations employing year-round labor. A 2007 Land Trust Alliance report found that farmers need around 12 seasonal workers during harvest time for a fifty-acre orchard. One larger operation hires near to 100. Mesa County alone hired 1,900 agricultural workers.[81]

Importing contract labor did not emerge as a practice until the expanding Western Slope sugar beet industry could not source enough local help. In "Valley of Opportunity," Steven F. Mehls writes about how the Holly Sugar Company looked south of the border.

> *Cowboys and farm hands refused the backbreaking work of thinning and pulling beets so growers hired children 11 to 15 years old as field workers. When this labor pool dried up, Mormons, German-Russians, Chinese, and Native Americans all were tried. Eventually, in 1916, [Hispanics] were brought in from Mexico by the Holly Sugar Company as contract laborers. Some members of this last group decided to stay and become permanent residents of the Grand Valley.[82]*

The seasonal—and more recently year-round—agricultural labor need on the Western Slope has historically drawn from a diverse pool of America's well-seasoned "melting pot." Native, African and Anglo Americans have all had a chapter in the story of the harvest. Asians who had pounded the iron ties of the country together also contributed to developing agriculture, though with a limited mark: they were severed from immigration opportunities with the passing of legislation in the late nineteenth century and into the twentieth with the Immigration Act of 1924.[83] German prisoners of war lent a temporary and tightly supervised hand to the orchardists. Mexican nationals had long been establishing themselves in the Southwest territories of North America, beginning with the 1910 Mexican Revolution and with an increasing exodus northward over the years for those seeking refuge from war.[84] They have become an integrated part of the culture on the Western Slope, and their contributions are inseparable from the success of the modern-day fruit harvest.

"[Migrant workers] are so valuable," says Palisade Chamber of Commerce executive director Juliann Adams. "They're a huge part of what goes on here. We wouldn't be able to do what we do without them."

Opposite, bottom: Hotchkiss-Crawford Historical Museum director and North Fork Valley author Kathy McKee's mother, Elsie, and grandfather Richard Hartman picking peaches on Rodger's Mesa circa 1938. *Photo courtesy Kathy McKee.*

New Roots

The initial ebb and flow of labor resources came primarily from the migrants homesteading on small farms. Boosters in Mesa County formed an immigration board in the 1890s to aid potential and new residents. An advisory group provided community connections to land, water, housing, bankers and merchants. Most of these newly established fruit ranchers had small, individual growing operations, due in part to the financial and labor demands of a start-up. The family nucleus managed most day-to-day chores, but once the fruit ripened on the trees, the community rallied to help. Time was the taskmaster as a crop—peaches more than apples—could hit the ground or became unsellable in as few as twenty-four hours. From neighbors to surrounding townships, every available man, woman and child picked fruit back then.[85] Labor demands continued. Once the fruit left the orchards, the packing sheds near the rail stations became temporary villages: girls and women handled the fruit, preparing it for transport; men nailed on the lids and loaded the crates onto the train cars.

It is a communal effort that, on a smaller scale, continued through the influx of migratory workers and into present day. Palisade Historical

For Jimmy Pascall (pictured) and other men, nailing boxes for shipping the fruit was a summer-long occupation. *Photo courtesy Z's Orchards.*

A fruit-packing crew that includes Hotchkiss-Crawford Historical Society volunteer Marilyn Tate's uncles Norval (second from left) and Leonard Bruce (far right). *Photo courtesy Marilyn Bruce Tate.*

Society founding chairman Priscilla Walker, whose grandfather settled in Palisade in 1893, speaks about harvest season during the middle of the twentieth century:

> *When I was growing up, peach harvest was an all-consuming effort for the Valley. Everyone, including youngsters, and thousands of migrant workers were needed to get the millions of Elberta peaches picked, packed and shipped in refrigerator box cars in three weeks in August...My first job was "box girl" at age six. I was in the top floor of the packing shed and shoved wooden boxes down a metal-edged chute so professional peach packers—who packed four hundred boxes of peaches a day, would have a box nearby when they needed it. I progressed to packer and, finally, "gate girl." In that job, I made sure the packers had enough of similar-size peaches to keep them constantly busy packing fruit. They wrapped each peach in tissue paper and placed it in a wooden box according to a pattern that minimized bruising during the trip in a refrigerated rail car to markets in the Midwest.*[86]

The need for additional hands at harvest season proliferated from the time of the early homeseeker as orchard sizes expanded. Grower representatives advertised the need for help in states like Arizona, Iowa and Wisconsin. An era of transient labor began in earnest with the mid-section of the country shrouded in the Dust Bowl.

ITINERANT ROOTS

When the Heartland was battered by drought and the Great Depression, families packed up their jalopies and headed west looking to survive. The Grand Valley was a migrant throughway for midwesterners with their hopes set on California. Some stayed to work, and some continued onward to the coast.[87]

While the influx of transient families added to the temporary workforce, unpredictability led to problems of experience, housing and labor surplus and shortages. This Americana migratory era fostered a nomadic culture labeled at the time as "fruit tramps." These field workers and their families journeyed around the country, traveling to locations based on the varying harvest schedules and, in some cases, returning year after year.[88]

As the Western Slope fruit culture rolled toward the 1940s, Roosevelt's New Deal provided some relief to those displaced by the Depression. The Resettlement Administration was designed to put the unemployed back into the workforce by giving them a boost into farming. Local offices in Fruita and Grand Junction helped more than three dozen transient families establish farms on public Grand Valley Reclamation tracts.[89] Another effort involved the building of Civilian Conservation Corps (CCC) camps. The corps built camps on previously owned or newly purchased public land in Delta, Fruita, Grand Junction and Palisade. The camp in the Palisade area along the Colorado River—Riverbend Park, home to the Peach Festival— housed temporary laborers in a two-hundred-unit facility while they worked in the fruit industry or for area water projects.[90]

WWII reversed the extremes of the Great Depression. From 1940 to 1945, crop values tripled.[91] Labor surplus turned to scarcity, and farmers looked toward migrant help. The Mesa County Peach Board of Control, an industry advocacy group for the Western Slope, created a committee public outreach campaign to solicit help. Leveraging patriotic loyalty, they asked community members to "help the war effort" by spending their vacation time assisting with harvest activities. In a broader reach, they went to Washington, D.C., to ask for help sourcing labor. Both pleas were effective. Colorado citizens responded, and government agency meetings led to aid from Hispanic farm

"Camp Mesa" Civilian Conservation Corps Camp BR-59-C in 1939 is now site of present-day Riverbend Park. *Photo courtesy Palisade Historical Society, Peska Family Collection.*

laborers, Japanese internees and German POWs,[92] the latter of which had been captured in Africa and imprisoned in Trinidad, Colorado. The POWs were transported to the Western Slope—Delta, Montrose, Fruita, Grand Junction and Palisade—to help with the harvests and were housed in groups of 250, primarily in the CCC camps.

In "Harvesting Peaches with German Prisoners of War," Grand Junction resident George Zimmerman chronicled the summer of '44, when he spent his vacation picking peaches alongside POWs:

> *The morning work at camp began when about fifteen or twenty trucks came in to pick up their prisoners. The German officers had them all counted out in groups according to the number each grower wanted and they were loaded up and on their way…At meal time [sic] the Germans would congregate on a small parade area, get into formation, and march while singing to the mess hall for meals…I had to get a report from each grower on the number of bushels picked by the prisoners to see that they were not loafing on the job or picking green fruit…One grower on Orchard Mesa got several cases of beer and served them at one of their breaks each day, and they picked more peaches per man for him than for any other.*[93]

Internees and POWs provided extra harvest hands until 1946. In later years, growers brought in significant numbers of African American pickers from the South. Dennis Clark remembers that in the early '60s his family

Migrant workers are valuable help to fruit-farming operations, especially during the peach harvest. *Photo courtesy High Country Orchards & Vineyards.*

American officials acted on the Geneva Convention articles noting that POWs could be used for labor. The United States utilized an estimated 375,000 Germans in the workforce from 1943 to 1946.[95]

hosted about thirty workers in their farmhouse. "We lived in the downstairs, and the upstairs was a kind of bunkhouse…with single beds across," Clark says. "I'd go up and play cards with them when I was a little kid and we'd cook for them downstairs on a big kitchen stove. Breakfast, lunch, and dinner. We roomed them all in the same house that we lived in. That's just the way it was."[94]

Navajos—and Sioux—labored in canneries and in the orchards but gravitated more to the beet and tomato fields. Whole families traveled together and, in some cases, worked alongside each other when farms hired them all. They would return to their homes, primarily reservations, for culturally important religious ceremonies like the Blessing Way. Unfortunately, for the farmers, these traditions did not always coincide with the needs of the harvest.

Transient labor on the Western Slope has had a diverse history, but the population with the greatest impact on the fruit culture is an amalgamation of those with Hispanic heritage.

KITCHEN CLOUT

The peach industry during and after the war in Western Colorado was booming, with one million bushels produced annually in the 1940s, requiring five to six thousand sets of hands to help each harvest.[96] The second generation Bracero Program, an agreement between Mexico and the United States to fill the void of agricultural workers due to WWII, opened the boarders in 1942. The agreement was Mexico's contribution to the war against the Axis powers. They intended it to last the duration of the war, but this "managed migration" program became law in 1951 and continued into 1964. The official agreement contained provisions of wages, room and board, as well as transportation and antidiscrimination. Regardless, this paperwork gateway did not always have open arms nor adhere to labor rights. Boarders were overwhelmed with unemployed Hispanics who came into the United States, both legally and undocumented, needing work to support their families. While most entered into Texas and California, many made their way to the Western Slope's fruit country.[97]

Mexican nationals and Americans stayed on the grower property and in the CCC camps. A report based on inspections by the National Child and Labor Committee found camps throughout Colorado unsanitary, adding, "To visitors, life in migrant quarters appeared to be one long spell of privation and misery." One of the two camps in the state rated "good" was the Palisade Migratory Labor Camp. In 1948, the Palisade Peach Board of Control took over the previously government-owned CCC camp along the Colorado River near town, which opened the doors to civilian aid. The camp was home, albeit meager and questionably suitable, to thousands during the federal and private ownership for a respective twenty years. It closed in the early 1960s. A few of the units were broken up and sold or moved to grower properties. Although some growers provided their workers with proper living quarters, until the mid-1990s, housing for migrants was, according to the state health department, "horrible." Families lived in campers, under bridges or in "overcrowded," "inadequate, unsafe and/or unaffordable housing."[98]

A kitchen-table tour de force of growers' wives led a grass-roots movement to change the substandard living conditions. The ringleaders included Dorothy Power, Ruby Toothacher, Vera Foss and her sister, the venerable Margaret Talbott. They gathered their respective feminine community collateral together on a mission to "alleviate the conditions of migratory workers in our vicinity." The Palisade Women's Club, the United Church Women of Palisade and the Colorado Council of Churches Migrant

Ministry joined in the collaboration. Led by the Palisade Women's Club, the group organized under one umbrella, becoming the Mesa County Migrant Council. Their first president, Margaret Talbott, took the helm, and they conducted their first meeting on November 17, 1955.[99]

The conditions the group addressed were essential human needs of food, shelter and clothing. Local civic groups like Future Farmers of America and Mesa County Public Health further supported improvement activities. Medical needs outreach extended into basic health, first aid and vaccination. The program added nutritional guidance with meal preparation instructions using low-cost ingredients that did not need refrigeration, as their temporary housing often had none. The council developed transportation, education, recreation and childcare programs, along with a thrift store that is still an important resource.[100]

The Mesa County Migrant Council eventually retitled as Child & Migrant Services (CMS). CMS operated their many services through the years out of a mobile health van, the Fruita Child Care Center, the Palisade Veterans building and a Hospitality Center trailer. Then, in 1989, aided by contributions from local resources and Colorado foundations, CMS purchased a historical building in Palisade—the Hospitality Center's current location. The site provides centralized access to their services and programs, including English as a Second Language (ESL) education and cultural orientation. "Workers that come from other countries face big cultural and language barriers," CMS director Karalyn Dorn says, adding that they feel like outsiders. "It's important to give them a place where they feel they belong."[101]

The center's tamale project is one way American and Hispanic cultures connect in the fruit community. With help from Collbran Job Corps training students, a small pool of volunteers and one primary chef, Maria Lopez, the kitchen crew makes seventy to eighty dozen tamales at a time, selling them (and selling out) to the public and pocketing a minimal profit for the program.

Off-site, CMS, area growers and migrant advocates' Talbott Farms orchestrated more stable housing for workers and their families. Together they built a thirty-bed housing development that earned Talbott Farms a prestigious Eagle Award by Housing Colorado and led to the construction of many more projects. CMS, too, facilitates an employee/employer connection. Employers hire foreign nationals through the H-2A work visa program—one laden with extensive paperwork on each end—for temporary agricultural help. Dorn says farms need to hire a huge number of workers for the peach harvest for a relatively short period of time. She adds, "It requires a lot of skill, knowledge and education…Many growers like to employ the same people because of their experience."

An economic research report from Mesa Land Trust stated that $12.4 million is spent on "hired labor" each year by agriculture operations, with over 1,900 laborers hired in 2007. Migrant workers are a significant percentage of the total. In 2014, migrants from Brazil, Italy, Japan and other countries came to work in the Grand Valley. Still, that does not mean

Orchardists like Arvid Muhr (right) walked on stilts while working in the orchard to move quickly between trees, especially for pruning. *Photo courtesy Z's Orchard.*

57

that hired labor does all the work. Most farms are fewer than five acres.[102] Sometimes, regardless of the acreage, there is just not enough help to go around. Plus, growers like Dennis Clark just like to keep working in the fields:

[Pruning season] *is a quiet time of the year. It's cold in the mornings and nice in the afternoon. You're out in the sunshine. Beautiful sky normally—it's that time of the year there's less going on. Today's phone is not ringing as often and as much…Training the tree and watching it develop—I've just always enjoyed that. I enjoy the prune.*

4

MOVEABLE MARKETS

I hope that this convention, before its final adjournment, will pass resolutions to be forwarded to the American Apple Congress…Make it a punishable offense to dispose of wormy and unsalable apples under a brand that would lead the purchaser to believe that they were otherwise. When we have accomplished this, a box of Colorado apples will represent an edition deluxe of the sweetest poems on earth.
—*Fred G. Shaffer,* Annual Report of the State Board of Horticulture, *1910*

Before produce could be transported by rail and truck and air from Western Slope farms to tables across the continent, and before urban agritourists began traveling to fields for a taste of u-pick, what grew or mooed in the field out back was *what's for supper*. New markets developed when miners—the first locavores—needed sustenance and when the Grand and North Fork Valleys' fruit fame spread eastward. The challenge for growers was getting the fruit to the consumers in the expected condition of excellence.

THE IRON TIES THAT BIND

Getting supplies into mountain communities or over the hump of the Continental Divide to the East was no easy trek: passable roads were not commonplace in the 1800s. With Western Colorado benefiting little from federal or state government aid, most road development funding came from private sources with a fiscal interest in town building. Road-building pioneers like Otto Mears and Enos Hotchkiss constructed routes through the Rockies that highway engineers today find barely feasible even with modern technology.[103]

One seemingly impassable route connecting the isolated Western Slope with markets in eastern counties and beyond was through the steep-sloped DeBeque Canyon (then Hogback Canyon) along the Colorado River. This more direct passage had the capacity to cut off over one hundred miles for cross-state travelers and goods. Builder Henry Rhone envisioned a dirt road

Roan Creek Toll Road—now I-70—in the days of Stagecoach travel circa 1885. *Photo courtesy Museum of Western Colorado, Lloyd Files Research Library.*

through the canyon—one with the potential for a profitable right-of-way sale to the railroad—that is now the paved course of heavily traveled I-70. By the end of 1885, after a few false starts and detours, transport of goods and people in and out of the Grand Valley went through the canyon on Rhone's Roan Creek Toll Road. County Commissioners set the rates: "Stagecoach, $3.00; each saddle animal, 75¢; loose cattle, horses and mules, 22½¢ each; loose hogs and sheep, 75¢ each."[104]

The toll road through the canyon improved access, but growers were still without a cross-continental fast track to distant consumers. Regionally, they turned to the "iron horse" rails that connected mountain mining communities with the outside world.

Spurs of the narrow gauge, and eventually the more stable standard gauge, connected Aspen silver, Leadville gold and the many Colorado coalfields to industry. Tracks ran through the valleys and along the foot of the Western Slope to the newly platted town of Delta, North Fork Valley's county seat, and the intersection of Denver & Rio Grande Railroad's (D&RG) main westward line in the Grand Valley.[105] The Board of Trade in Grand Junction, a chamber of commerce for the Western Slope, put out an 1889 circular championing the links, stating, "Markets for Grand Valley fruit are all the principal cities and mining camps of the state…The opening of the new broad gauge road to Aspen and Leadville will add to the facilities for disposing of all that can be grown here."[106]

Railroad companies and their investors clamored to be the first to reach prospecting communities. A transcontinental link—their mother lode—joining Rifle and Grand Junction rail ends, however, had yet to meet. Competitors Colorado Midland Railway (CMR) and the D&RG had been racing each other in the Roaring Fork and Colorado River Valleys. They eventually combined forces, completing the much-desired coast-to-coast network in 1890.[107]

Growers in Mesa and Delta Counties had a method of getting their products to markets. Still, unless their orchard was near to the mining community lines, they had a long trek to load it onto the railcars. North Fork farmers at the high, far end of the valley needed to haul their fruit up to forty miles down to Delta, the shipping nucleus for the region. For almost twenty years, farmers drove horse-drawn wagons heaped with apples or peaches down dirt roads to the railroad docks, with the dust trail visible for miles.[108] Then, in 1902, the Rio Grande Delta, an offshoot of the D&RG, completed the North Fork line: a branch that joined Delta to Hotchkiss and Paonia.

The popular heart-shaped Red Delicious apple cultivar began as a "chance seedling" on an Iowa farm in the late 1800s. *Author photo.*

Beginning in 1910, an electric interurban line called the Fruit Belt ran from Grand Junction to Fruita and back, connecting orchard bounty with consumers. Fruita residents were also ecstatic to have a metropolis connection. Accessibility spurred a boom of growth and development. Fruit Belt publicity booklets encouraged visitors to take sightseeing train trips past the orchards or "stop and buy land." In addition to goods and tourists, the electric rail transported Fruita residents and schoolchildren. "In late summer when it was hot we'd have the window down and the car would bump the apple branches and the kids would reach out and grab an apple," remembers Wilma Shaw in *The Fruit Belt Route* historical book publication, adding, "But if Clyde Scoles caught them they'd have trouble." Years later, a five-and-a-half-mile extension, the Peavine, reached out from Fruita into the fields, running a less romantic and more utilitarian transportation with convenient loading of the potatoes and sugar beets that usurped the fruit in crop dominance.[109]

Even with the improved means of transporting fruit to expanding markets, in order to maintain quality standards, fruit shipped long distances through the heat required special railroad cars. D&RG modified boxcars for perishables early on with ventilation and double-insulated walls flanked on the ends with ice compartments. They used interchangeable trucks, or

Fruit Belt Route electric interurban rail circa 1910. *F.E. Dean photograph courtesy of Library of Congress.*

wheel assemblies, so that the cars could transition back and forth over their standard and narrow-gauge rails. The CMR Company developed cars able to ship sixty thousand pounds with center-bunker ice compartments.

Ice for the refrigerated cars, or "reefers," was not manufactured—it was harvested in midwinter from Rocky Mountain lakes and ponds. Workers scored the ice with rotary saws, or used horse-drawn plows with runners that etched a grid pattern. Next, they cut out blocks of ice in sections. Harvesters then prodded and floated the sections toward shore. The individual blocks were either loaded onto wagons or stacked into train cars for delivery to icehouses, or stations. Workers transferred the ice into reefers, loading it into hatches on top of the cars. The North Fork Fruit Growers' Association's packing/shipping shed on the D&RG branch utilized a Paonia station with ice from a local pond. Delta had a couple of icehouses. Grand Junction, Western Colorado's railway hub, had at least four. Their ice was harvested from up to 150 miles away: above Minturn and outside of Kremmling. Both private organizations and railroad companies maintained approximately 120 icing stations along the freight routes throughout the state.[110]

Builders constructed early houses with dirt or concrete floors and tar roofs. For insulation, sawdust covered the ground, was packed between the ice blocks and filled the walls inside the wooden structures. Over the span of thirteen years, three fires destroyed icehouses in Grand Junction, beginning in 1918 with the largest in the city's history that also burned the freight depot. No one knows what started the devastating 1918 fire, but two weeks prior, a fire had flared in nearly the same site. Fires were not uncommon in those days. The St. Regis Hotel (refurbished Grand Hotel), St. Mary's Hospital and Hampton General Store, as well as greenhouses and numerous packing sheds, caught fire. Causes ranged from explosions to overworked heating systems to transient fruit tramps.[111]

Ice harvesting near Paonia. *Photo courtesy of Denver Public Library, Western History Collection [Call # X-12958].*

Icehouses rebuilt in Grand Junction included more efficient methods and machines. They implemented uniform block size for storage to eliminate wasted space, along with mechanical elevators and automatic loaders that minimized human handling and expedited the transfer into the reefers. This new and improved generation of icehouse had a storage capacity of thirty-three thousand tons.[112]

The Edison Film Company created a slide presentation about Grand Valley fruit farming that was shown as far away as Madison Square Garden in 1910. It was an effort supported by the Grand Junction Chamber of Commerce to help spread the word to distant markets.[113]

BEASTS OF BURDEN

Reefers, transcontinental rails and additional branches all improved the growers' ability to supply fresh fruit to an increasingly larger group of consumers. In spite of this—and sometimes because of it—farmers were met with additional challenges. Picking, packing and transportation strained railroad company means as well as human capabilities. Ice, railcars and labor needs did not always match available resources. Prices fluctuated. Crops fell in and out of favor. Deeply rooted resident of the North Fork Valley and Hotchkiss-Crawford Historical Museum liaison Marilyn Bruce Tate explains:

> *When the train got up* [to Paonia] *then* [workers] *could load cars…they ordered cars ahead of time for the fruit and then loaded it…sometimes they would not get enough cars so their fruit would have to sit. Some years they lost a lot of money because they couldn't get their fruit out. And, too, they would get their fruit on the trains and the trains would sit in the heat and the fruit would spoil.*[114]

Growers banded together early on to try to tame the unpredictable beast, forming the Grand Junction Fruit Growers' Association in 1891. They worked together to manage supply, storage and shipping, as well as to control rates. Over the next few decades, more co-ops formed on the Western Slope:

Hotchkiss Fruit Company shed and crew circa 1905–06. *Photo courtesy Hotchkiss-Crawford Historical Society.*

North Fork Fruit Growers' Association, Colorado Fruit Growers' Association, Palisade Peach Growers' Association and Fruita Fruit and Produce.

In addition, co-ops constructed packing and shipping sheds with loading docks at various locales along the tracks to help unite distribution efforts. Having a central location enabled workers to inspect, pack and promptly load fruit into the ice-accommodating cars.[115] Co-ops also supported community efforts to construct evaporating plants for drying fruit and canneries for the management of overripe and surplus stock.[116] In 1904, Paonia's Nelson Brothers' Fruit Company shipped 283 railcars of fruit, and the North Fork Fruit Growers Association processed 136 cars of peaches and 160 of apples.[117] At peak peach harvests, Palisade would send out over 100 railcars of fruit per day. The D&RG and Colorado Midland team that had once blazed the path of progress was now playing catch-up with the

expanding fruit market, having to borrow cars from other lines in 1910 to transport the abundant crops.

With Colorado's passing of the Co-operative Marketing Act in 1923, a co-op could operate in a similar fashion as a corporation. This meant exclusive contracts and better capital management. This same year, the United Fruit Growers' Association of Palisade formed, viewed by many as the most "cooperative" of the associations. By using promissory notes from growers rather than stock and by paying for supplies with cash, they were able to receive discounts and levy charges, as well as distribute revenue returns to members with the excess.[118]

The co-ops, by and large, campaigned in the best interests of their members. Others, however, operated with their own set of standards—a factor that Palisade Historical Society founding chairperson Priscilla Bowman Walker says was "the eight-hundred-pound gorilla in the room."[119] In addition, some charged excessive handling fees or ended up competing

Tour de Vineyards cyclists riding the twenty-five-mile Palisade Fruit & Wine Byway loop during Winefest pass a historical packing shed. *Author photo*.

with each other, impairing the welfare of growers. Neither did associations always operate on the up and up. Over time, some collapsed or were absorbed by larger packinghouses and even restructured to regain grower control.

"People started peddling out the back door," explains Harry Talbott, a Palisade peach magnate whose parents settled in the area in the early twentieth century. "Self-inflicted wounds caused the eventual demise of the co-op."[120]

SHADE HATS AND PARASOLS

The fruit culture no longer required centralized effort as transportation evolved and as growers became more self-sufficient. Specialty store markets for Western Slope fruit evolved with the advent of retailers like Natural Grocers and Whole Foods. Direct sales, too, have increased: farmers' markets across Colorado in the mid-1980s redefined the renaissance to meet contemporary lifestyles; community supported agriculture (CSA) programs—a co-op culture for the new millennium that is less about shipping and more about sharing—create a risk/reward kinship between members and farmers; agritourists, a rising direct-sale demographic, combine travel with a taste for fresh.

The Colorado Farm Fresh Guide (print, with mobile "app-Apple" and Android versions) points consumers toward u-pick opportunities, roadside

Above: The Golden Route on the West Elk Scenic and Historic Byway in the North Fork Valley is a stretch of inviting farm markets, wineries and art galleries. *Author photo.*

Right: Garvin Mesa in Paonia is home to Stone Cottage Cellars, Azura Cellars & Gallery, Desert Weyr and Terror Creek Winery, with Black Bridge Winery and market at its foot. *Author photo.*

The quaint sign pointing to Terror Creek Winery is a reflection of the valley. *Author photo.*

stands and farmers' markets, as well as festival listings and over two hundred unpretentious farms.

Just off the Golden Route of the West Elk Scenic and Historic Byway in the North Fork Valley, it's families-meet-*farm stays* for vacations with a rural reconnect. Urbanites escape to places like Mesa Winds Farm, where they can stay in a "picker cabin" and, if they choose, roll up their sleeves and help in the harvest. At bed-and-breakfasts like Fresh & Wyld, visitors don gardening and chef hats for classes on preparing farm-to-table feasts. There are roadside stands and country stores like Black Bridge Winery and Delicious Orchards.

In the Grand Valley, the Palisade Fruit & Wine Byway is a twenty-five-mile loop past fruit farms on lettered (north–south) and numbered (east–west) roads that step and bend past orchards and vineyards, stands and stores. Bicyclists pedal past peach trees and cabernet grapes, stopping for sustenance at markets like Anita's Pantry and Produce. Motorists bring shopping lists, coolers and corks for their county road excursions. Growers like Sage Creations Organic Farm hand out parasols during the Lavender Festival to shade the strollers from the intense sun. Agritourists walk or ride golf carts on orchard tours with growers, seeing firsthand the story of fruit farming—a reintroduction of food to consumer. The humble, quiet life of the farm is now open to the public.

5

WESTWARD FLOW

Here is a land where life is written in Water; the West is where the Water was
and is; Father and Son of old Mother and Daughter.
—Poet Thomas Hornsby Ferril, Colorado State Capitol building, circa 1940

There can be no agricultural heartbeat on the Western Slope without two primary water sources: the Gunnison, and the state's namesake, the Colorado.

The path of the Colorado River from past to present day is one that influenced settlement from the Grand Valley of Colorado to the Imperial Valley in California.[121] Although this aquatic lifeline shaped the pioneers' ability to put down roots in the soil of arid landscapes, humans have in turn sculpted the progression of the river. Engineers of ancient and modern cultures created diversions, dams and ditches to control water flow for agricultural irrigation, flood management and urbanite domestic usage. Irrigated acre values are in the billions from Colorado to California.[122] With so much at stake, it's no wonder the story of the Colorado River is a Western tale filled with adventure, conquests and wrangling.

COLORADO RIVER: THE LIFE BLOOD

The saga of the Colorado River that affects the borders of the Grand Valley begins not at the humble headwaters on La Poudre Pass on the Continental

Divide or at its dehydrated end near the Gulf of California. This 1,400-mile (give or take, depending on dam releases and beginning point of measurement)[123] story begins with a name.

Historians credit Franciscan Spaniard Father Garcés with naming the river when he crossed it near Moab, Utah, below the confluence with the Green River while on his way to California in 1776.[124] A phenomenon due to the surrounding sandstone geology that affects the water's color inspired the name "Rio Colorado." The flow from the Utah confluence to its origins on La Poudre Pass in Colorado—where French fur trappers and mountain men like Kit Carson first breached the area for trade—was originally called the Grand River, labeled perhaps by the French.[125]

The "father of Western Slope water rights,"[126] Congressman Edward T. Taylor, contended in 1921 that this section be renamed Colorado, arguing that although the Green is longer, the Grand is the "main stream of the Colorado" because it contributes "twenty-five percent more water."[127] Some fought for "Grand," as namesakes already included a ditch, lake, town (Grand Junction in Mesa County) and county, but Taylor's argument won over. Thus the river became the "Colorado" from headwater to gulf.

Under both identities, this mighty stream and the Gunnison River have been, and are, diverted, dammed and pumped agricultural lifelines.

Grand Valley's pre-irrigation landscape for early settlers. *Photo courtesy Grand Valley Water Users' Association, Grand Junction, CO.*

72

THE IRRIGATION EVOLUTION

Agricultural techniques that channel water to parched fields and enable farmers to cultivate are not the invention of nineteenth-century man's ingenuity. Irrigation as a practice—its laws literally written in stone—goes back to the days of Babylon.[128] In the West, irrigation history credits the handiwork of ancient Anasazi Indians, who, in the view of archaeologist Jerry Spangler, "thrived in the deserts like no other people before or since."[129]

An exploration of southwest Colorado by Corps of Topographical Engineers captain J.N. Macomb that began in 1859 found "traces of [ancient] irrigation ditches."[130] Numerous curious adventurers and their surveys followed, with findings that included dams and reservoirs.[131] The Anasazi may have been the first in Colorado to irrigate, but in 1852, the first irrigation rights granted by the government went to Spanish Americans on the Eastern Slope, whose knowledge originated with the Moor Invasion centuries earlier in Spain.[132]

The greatest impact on agricultural development in Colorado, however, came from the Anglo-Americans who looked westward for natural resources. Colorado's Front Range served as a gateway to gold and led to settlement in what explorer Major Stephen H. Long mapped out as the "Great American Desert." These semiarid eastern plains were not the hoped for Jeffersonian "farmer's garden" but the implementation of irrigation practices in the last half of the nineteenth century that transformed land along the ditches into cultivatable parcels. Veins of canals traced back from the fields to western agriculture's end of the rainbow: water.

Water from the ten to twenty-plus annual feet of accumulated mountain snow melts off each side of the Continental Divide and travels down multiple tributaries.[133] East of the divide, they merge into three primary rivers: the Rio Grande, the Arkansas and the Platte. The Colorado River flows west.

The public knew little of the Colorado River until John Wesley Powell's river explorations and U.S. Geological Survey of the Territories leader F.V. Hayden's geological and topographical expedition surveys provided insight to its nature and agricultural value. Powell's information determined that the river ways coming out of the mountains were "unnavigable" and were therefore serviceable for agriculture. Hayden's team—comprised of botanists, geologists and topographers—reported on the Grand Valley's agricultural potential. Powell supported water use for irrigation, and Hayden endorsed its necessity.[134] Homeseekers emigrating from the East, as well as lawmakers, needed to rethink western water management.

The 100th meridian running roughly down the midline of the country divides the humid, stream-saturated garden lands of the East from the dry plains and plateaus of the West. According to the Colorado Water Conservation Board, agriculture in general requires annual precipitation of twenty inches.[135] The Western Slope valleys average well below the minimum at eight to fourteen inches. Early farmers and fruit ranchers could not function under the same riparian laws as the East: eastern doctrine limited proprietary rights to those with bordering land to limit impact on flow needed for navigation and mill power.

The Doctrine of Prior Appropriation, written into state charter in 1876 and adopted by seven other western states, established a "first in time, first in right" law. The Colorado Division of Water Resources offers a simplified explanation, stating, "This system of water allocation controls who uses how much water, the types of uses allowed, and when those waters can be used…The first person to appropriate water and apply that water to [beneficial] use has the first right to use that water within a particular stream system."[136]

Western Slope township founders George Crawford and William E. Pabor understood irrigation and its importance to transforming the Grand Valley into a fruitful landscape. Fruita founder William E. Pabor highlights irrigation in his 1883 book *Colorado as an Agricultural State*, writing about the emerging practice with the inclusion of mathematical volume equations, rules for diversion methods and estimates of arable acres per region. Pabor summates irrigation's importance to Colorado agriculture: "To write about Colorado agriculture and say nothing concerning irrigation, would be like enacting the play of Hamlet, leaving out the principal character therein."[137]

A DITCH RUNS THROUGH IT

Taming the water was originally up to those who wanted and needed it in both the Grand and North Fork Valleys, including flood control in addition to irrigation for the latter. The North Fork of the Gunnison River flows into a valley surrounded on three sides by the Grand Mesa, Gunnison River Canyons and the West Elk Mountains. Heavy spring snowmelt, especially when aided by rain, caused many floods over the years destroying orchards and buildings. Early settlers built dikes, diversions and ditches to try to harness the power and potential.

Ditches are part of an old and intricate irrigation system that hydrates the fruit and wine crops on the Western Slope. *Author photo.*

Farmers in both valleys whose fields were next to water sources dug dirt ditches, or furrows, to guide water to their crops. Some created jointly operated ditches where neighbors ran their water from the same "mother ditch" instead of each person furrowing to the river. Those whose property— or township residence—did not benefit from accessible creeks or streams hauled water out of the river prior to a canal system. Orchardists who needed water for more than domestic chores used teams of horses to haul barrels back and forth, up and down long stretches of dirt roads every two to three weeks.

Therefore, ditch companies organized, developing networks of systems that changed this intensive labor. However, ditch delivery was neither clean nor efficient. Losses from seepage were an estimated 60–70 percent.[138] In spite of bringing water sources a little closer to home and field, ditches were a murky deal: overflow onto the streets, "filthy" and foul smelling and almost immediately insufficient. In a *Journal of Western Slope* publication, the daughter of an early inhabitant of rural Western Colorado recounted her mother's resourcefulness on washday:

> *In summer, if the ditch water was muddy when wash day came, Myrtle would take a few prickly pear cactus, burn the spines off, pound the cactus into a mass with a hammer, and then stir it into a barrel of water. In a few minutes, the juice of the cactus would absorb mud out of the water and settle to the bottom of the barrel, leaving the water clear.[139]*

As settlement and agriculture expanded in Colorado, larger and more organized, expensive systems were needed. The drivers of establishing this network were developers and the media. The *Rocky Mountain News* flexed its circulation muscles in an 1864 editorial that "urged upon the present Congress," to consider a plan that would "grant a portion of the public domain" for the construction of canals.[140] Within the text they laid out the idea for a law that would eventually become the Reclamation Act of 1902.

In 1881, men started work on the Grand Valley Ditch, hacking a path in the ground with picks and shovels intended to run twelve miles in length and through land on which they had yet to file a claim. Ground broke for the Pioneer Ditch the following year. Early peach farmer J.P. Harlow and Grand Junction founder George Crawford, along with a group of other local men, were instrumental in its development and eventual incorporation in 1884. Crawford was the primary financer of the next project, the Pacific Slope Ditch, his Grand Junction Township's water source. The Independent Ranchman's Ditch followed, but the project was lambasted by the press, as some believed its construction resources were in competition with the yet to be completed granddaddy canal, the Grand Valley Ditch. The granddaddy ditch (thirty-eight feet wide on the bottom, three to five feet deep, nine-plus miles long) went through years of wrangling and financial woes until 1895, when it was free of obstructions.[141]

Money to build the ditches ebbed and flowed. Companies formed, changed hands, expanded and reorganized. Private investors and ditch companies built canals with men, horses, blasting, digging and scraping. Ditches were "puddled" and lined with silt to slow saturation. Craftsmen built wooden flumes and head gates; floods tore them down. At the turn of the century, the canals were reinforced with steel and stone.

"What they built one hundred years ago is still working!" Orchard Mesa Irrigation District (OMID) manager Max Schmidt says. "The river siphons are still in the original concrete-lined channels from 1913. The siphons are PVC now and we've wore out pumps, but the system still works." Schimdt says OMID is only on its third generation of pumps that do a lot of heavy lifting. The pumps are hydraulic—they run on water instead of electricity—and each of the four pumps lifts 450 gallons per minute, or the equivalent of one ton of water per second.[142]

OMID is part of a network of six irrigation districts in Mesa County that deliver to over eighty thousand irrigated acres and the many head gates, after which irrigation management responsibilities become the landowners'. The districts are separately managed with different service areas, occasionally borrowing water from the Grand Valley Irrigation Company (GVIC). Schmidt says that the lending was "agreed upon with a one-hundred-year-old handshake until 1996." The legalities now "fill a thick three-ring binder." Even though the source of their water comes from the Colorado and the Gunnison Rivers, Schmidt says, "Every canal [district] is their own micro-system…canals are exactly the same, but different."[143]

One difference in particular is OMID diverts their water from above rather than below the diversion dam in DeBeque Canyon.

ROLLING ON THE RIVER

The one-hundred-year-old diversion dam on the Colorado River—known by locals as the "Roller Dam"—is a unique feature of a transformational and massive water control system constructed under the Grand Valley Project. The project was one of six initial works set into motion by the (Theodore) Roosevelt administration's Newland Reclamation Act of 1902 to foster prosperity and growth. Through the act, land that had been previously opened for settlement was returned to the government in sixteen semiarid/arid western states and territories for the purpose of water "storage, diversion, and development."[144] In a December message to Congress later that same year, President Roosevelt wrote:

> *Few subjects of more importance have been taken up by Congress…than the inauguration of the system of nationally-aided irrigation for the arid regions of the far west…The sound and steady development of the West depends upon the building of homes therein…One hundred and sixty acres of fairly rich and well-watered soil, or a much smaller amount of irrigated land, may keep a family in plenty, whereas no one could get a living out of one hundred and sixty acres of dry pasture land.[145]*

Reclamation gave communities the capital backing needed for large-scale projects, with payback strings attached. Without government funds, large-scale irrigation was cost and expertise prohibitive even for those with deep pockets. Wyoming's "Buffalo Bill" Cody transferred his water rights to capitalize on the act, as did "Billy the Kid" killer Sherriff Pat Garrett with his rights in New Mexico.[146] Less notable but financially able private interests from Chicago on Colorado's Western Slope were slower to relinquish control. The Grand Valley Project stalled in water disputes as a result. It regained momentum in 1907 through advocacy by the Grand Junction Chamber of Commerce, unanimous support in a citizen's meeting and a second $50,000 reclamation allocation in 1909.

While providing a significant boost, government resources waned, and shortcomings hindered progress. The Grand Valley Water Users' Association—formed as part of the project—proposed a membership dollar and labor contribution with a government match to expedite construction. Regardless, there were continuing rights-of-way concerns that held up project buy-in. Rights-of-way concerned both the farmers and the railroad. Growers wanted to protect orchard revenue from canal systems that required tree removal on their property. The Rio Grande Junction Railway wanted to protect its tracks from high-water damage. After years of concessions and redesigns, negotiations finally came close to resolution. Work began in 1912.

Land was excavated for the canals and tunnels. The tunnels were shored with wood and then lined with concrete that was protected with manure in cold weather while it set. Greek employees of the railroad raised the tracks five feet using the excavated dirt. And the United States contracted with the German firm Machinenfabrik Augsburg Nurnberg A.G. to design and construct a roller crest dam until WWI conflicts severed the relationship.

Reclamation engineer Fred Teichman took over the design, planning it after a European engineering concept. The fabrication contract went to a Pittsburgh manufacturing company. The end result was a fourteen-foot-high concrete wall running the width of the river. The height or crest of the water is managed with six seventy-foot-long tooth-rimmed rollers that are raised and lowered in varying combinations to achieve consistent water levels. Along with a sixty-foot sluiceway (spillway) controlled by an additional smaller gate, the design protects the railroad from flooding and enables passage of large debris over the crest. Orchard Mesa Siphon directs water underneath the river above the dam for their district while water below flows into the Government High Line Canal and into additional ditches. All combined, the system built by 750 men extends 90.1 miles at a cost of approximately $4.5 million. At the time it was constructed, it was the largest roller crest dam in the world.[147]

The Grand Valley Diversion Dam in DeBeque Canyon. *Photo courtesy Colorado River District.*

YOURS, MINE AND THEIRS

Fact: one thousand gallons of water are needed to produce and process each pound of food a person consumes annually. The investment per individual is 1.5 million gallons of water.[148] And that's just for agriculture. Multiple uses of irrigation, drilling and fracking, drinking, washing, landscaping, electricity and recreation—a main draw of Western Colorado—make water from the Colorado River a liquid treasure, an asset shared by nineteen states and Mexico.

Teams of stakeholders could not agree on fair water entitlements when development spread westward in the beginning of the twentieth century. Colorado and bordering states engaged in multiple litigations, challenging water distribution. The arid West looked to Colorado for hydration in the 1920s. Secretary of Commerce Herbert Hoover stepped in to mediate, recommending water of the Colorado River Basin be divided into upper and lower sections to protect development interests in the seven western states of both basin regions. The 1922 Colorado River Compact, an agreement the Bureau of Reclamation (BOR) characterizes as the "cornerstone" water law, became the rulebook that outlined Colorado River Basin states' apportionment and equity. Over the years, multiple regional, state, national and international laws affecting the Colorado River have been adopted and rewritten, rivers dissected and redirected.

Water regulations are a still a moving target. The 2013 Colorado Basin Roundtable Whitepaper notes:

> We face no less a crisis in water today than the pioneers faced in the late 1800s. Yet the needs, values, technologies and social structure of Colorado have changed considerably since 1876. We must not be afraid to reach beyond the boundaries of tradition to create real and sustainable solutions.[149]

Yet pressures on water supplies are not just from basin states downstream from Mesa County: Western Slope water sources like the Colorado and Gunnison Rivers provide for 80 percent of Colorado's water, while 80 percent of the population lives on the Eastern Slope. Trans-Mountain diversions channel a portion of western water under the Rockies to the east through tunnels and ditches, augmenting the Arkansas, South Platte and Rio Grande Basin sources that finger out of Colorado into Wyoming, Kansas, New Mexico and beyond. Approximately 70 percent of the Colorado River alone is obligated to leave its headwater state.

With predicted shortfalls of "greater than 3.2 million acre-feet by 2060"[150] and with rising populations in the West, the story of water will continue to be written and rewritten.

Wayne Aspinall Unit of the Colorado River Storage Project on the Gunnison River provides flood control benefits through water storage on three dams. Congressman Aspinall, initially in the Palisade peach industry and later widely known as a western water reclamation advocate, is famously quoted for his journalist John Gunther paraphrase: "In the West, when you touch water, you touch everything."

6
THE BUZZ

Clouds of insects danced and buzzed in the golden autumn light, and the air was full of the piping of the song-birds.
—Sir Arthur Conan Doyle, The White Company, *1891*

From birds to bees, from bears to bugs, Western Colorado's fields are populated with enemies and allies. Some of these foes and friends were immigrants, not native to the western part of the state's slope and valley ecosystem. Birds imported from Europe were some of the first winged pests. They cruise the skies in flocks, searching for unprotected bounty in Palisade vineyards. Conversely, orchards and fields of the Grand and North Fork Valleys are alive with pollinators, busying themselves in productive enterprises. Insects with both beneficial and detrimental impact swarm the Western Slope. Then, of course, there are the bears…

WINGED INTRUDERS

Around 1891, New York bird and Shakespeare fanatic Eugene Schieffelin took Shakespeare's words "I'll have a starling" from *Henry IV* off the page, bringing them to life and into North America. Schieffelin was the founder of the Acclimation Society, "whose goal was to introduce non-native species that they deemed culturally or environmentally beneficial into new

Starlings search for fruit at Colorado Cellars. *Author photo.*

environments."[151] The result of his attempt to import feathered icons of English skies and Shakespearian works became nothing short of a starling invasion. What began as sixty pairs in the east multiplied into 200 million birds from coast to coast and beyond international borders, making the starling the most common bird in North America. While Schieffelin did achieve his cultural goal, starlings have proven to be more destructive than advantageous to fruit farmers on the Western Slope.

This is in part due to the fact that starlings truly do "flock together": Communal roosting in trees causes breakage on young plantings; they devour fruit, with an impact of an estimated $800 million in annual damage to agriculture and property nationwide.[152] The *Colorado Grape Growers Guide* notes how flocks of starlings, along with other species—especially blackbirds—are attracted to ripening grapes and can cause significant damage in as little as thirty minutes.

Before the black-winged incursion spread fully westward, the raider in the sky was the robin. State Agriculture College professor W.W. Cooke shared his views on this outlaw in the Relation of Birds to Horticulture portion of the 1898 agricultural report:

> *It is not strange that in making the law they should mention the robin first. I think the horticulturist could make a very severe arraignment of the robin,*

more severe than of all other birds put together. I doubt if the other birds altogether eat as much fruit as the robins…there are thousands and tens of thousands of robins that go on stealing fruit. It is quite common to hear it said that during the time of year when fruit is plenty, the food of the robin is particularly fruit, and therefore its damage is more than its advantage. [153]

Despite their appetite for ripe fruit—and who can blame them—it was not the feathered foes that have caused the most damage and changed the course of fruit history on the Western Slope. It was another airborne creature that first made its unwelcome introduction to the region in that same 1898 report: the codling moth. Mesa County Horticultural Inspector B.F. Hughes noted in his annual report that a warm, wet fall followed by a severe winter led to atmospheric conditions that weakened the trees and contributed to an increase in insect populations. He singles out the codling moth, saying that it "appeared in many orchards for the first time and in such numbers as to destroy a portion of the apple crop." [154] (The Delta County inspector made no mention of the codling moth in his report, only the weather damage.)

For years, the codling moth continued to be the subject of entomology investigations. The 1921 *Life History of the Codling Moth in the Grand Valley of Colorado* deemed it as "the most serious insect pest attacking the fruit of the apple and pear." [155] Insect pests traveled to the West sans their natural predators on the same transportation rails as the immigrants, arriving on the train in recycled packing barrels and boxes. [156] The moths thrived in the Colorado climate. They nestled in orchard refuse, propagating their numbers. Insecticides were moderately effective, but the lead arsenate spray had to be washed off before it could be shipped—a process that damaged the quality of the thin-skinned apples and pears. Because of the codling moth, in addition to poor irrigation drainage practices, by the end of the 1920s, the apple industry on the Western Slope essentially ceased, especially in the once productive area of Fruita.

SECRET AGENTS

While the West has a geological force field—namely its semiarid climate—that helps to protect fruit from eastern enemies such as brown rot, scurfy scale and the weevil curculio, known for its assaults on apples and peaches, [157] the region is not impervious to pest infiltration, as the codling moth's destruction proved.

A grasshopper infestation on the Eastern Slope prompted a statewide investigation of insect defense strategies by the secretary of war in 1875 that went beyond the use of sprays. A Commission of Entomologists followed, with subsequent legislation that created their umbrella office: the State Board of Horticulture, establishing entomology as "perhaps the oldest Agriculture Regulatory Service of the State [of Colorado]"[158] and beginning the biological foresight that affected Colorado's leadership in the organic movement.[159]

The government entomologists looked to biological warfare to thwart the enemies that caused economic devastation, eventually recruiting special beneficial insects or "agents" to the task. Their mission? To combat threats that came openly and covertly into the Western Slope from Russia, China and exotic locales, as well as the eastern United States.

Successful field research using agents in Colorado began during the mid-1920s to help control the codling moths. Entomologists discovered that a parasitic wasp smaller than a pinhead, code name *Trichogramma minutum*, was an effective moth killer. Sometimes working in tandem with the parasitizing agent was an alluring sidekick that seduced the enemy into confusion: scent. Orchardists hung up an aromatic concoction of fermented juice infused with a chemical in wide-mouth jars that attracted the moth, luring it into the death trap.[160] Agents, used in combination with spraying methods, helped to significantly reduce the codling moth's scope of damage.

Beneficial insects could not help the Western Slope fruit industry when they suffered yet another blow in the 1930s from the peach mosaic virus, a setback that was perhaps more devastating than the Great Depression. The quick-spreading virus—a deforming disease spread by mites—affected every age and variety. Crews working for the State Bureau of Plant and Insect Control surveyed and inspected area orchards. They ordered virus-infected trees cut down and burned from root to trunk. Only complete eradication and quarantine could ensure the disease would not spread to healthy trees, so even young trees with minimal evidence were chopped down, flamed and removed. The virus severely wounded an already vulnerable peach industry. It pitted bureau crews against local orchardists, who did not want their livelihood to go up in smoke. In some of these instances, law enforcement had to step in to enforce the eradication. Local crewmembers were sensitive to the growers, including one who found the job "heart-sickening."[161] A Colorado Department of Agriculture's Code of Regulations report tallied the destruction in Mesa County: 32,163 infected trees destroyed by 1935, over 125,000 in total by 1964. Ultimately, the government and most growers ended up becoming allies on "the war" on insects, one they described as a "total war with no Armistice."[162]

The next threat on the horizon opened the doors of the Palisade Insectary. The Oriental fruit moth, aka OFM, was public enemy number one for peach growers. An organized group of growers who formed the Mesa County Peach Marketing Order, an industry oversight board, supported the recommendation of State of Colorado entomologist F. Herbert Gates to install an insectary. Affectionately called The Bug House, the insectary opened its lab in 1945 with the task of rearing and distributing an OFM natural predator. They raised the *Macrocentrus ancylivorus*, nicknamed "Mac." The Mac is a tiny, unassuming-looking female wasp that stings and eats OFM larvae. She was thriving in the lab and ready for her fieldwork by 1946. She immediately proved she had an effective on-the-job appetite.

The success of the "Mac Program gave biocontrol its first gold star," says insectary manager Dan Bean. Although, he adds, they are not a classic example of biocontrol, as they do not survive through the winter. As a result, the Palisade Insectary releases about 1½ to 2 million Macs each year. In the years since inception, the insectary has also developed biocontrol programs that mitigate invasive insects and weeds, such as the water-sucking allelopathic tamarisk. Bean

Netting draped over row after row of vines is the most effective method of thwarting throngs of hungry winged intruders used by modern-day viticulturists. *Author photo.*

European varieties of *Vitis vinifera* were susceptible to the *Grape Phylloxera* (root-eating insect) that resulted in the infestation and destruction of nearly 70 percent of Europe's vineyards, especially those of France's Rhône Valley. Entomologists grafted every European vine with phylloexera-resistant American rootstock, reviving Europe's wine industry.[163]

explains how typical beneficial insects operate: "You release the agent, it establishes, remains in the field, does its thing and after a certain number of releases—a certain amount of nurturing, we can walk away."

And although he isn't an "agent," Colorado State University Tri River Area Extension entomologist Bob Hammon is beneficial to the growers. Bean says that "farmers are pretty well on the lookout," and they send Hammon photos of suspicious-looking bugs to determine if they are a threat. "Hammon has his feelers out," says Bean, "and knows all the threats to Western Slope agriculture."

Au Naturel

Beneficial insects were agents of change for the biological era, prompting a shift back to the past, but not in the tradition of "let nature take its course." Natural and organic farming practice in Colorado is not a renaissance. It is more than releasing *a bag of bugs* in the orchards and hand-pulling weeds. It is an evolution with historic roots that predates wartime chemicals and with a present derived of ongoing research and technology.

The Ela family in Hotchkiss, who have been fruit farming in Western Colorado for four generations, have transitioned from conventional to environmental agriculture. Ela even had an uncle who was one of the researchers participating in early Orchard Mesa studies of the pest. "In one hundred years of farming we have farmed just about every way you can grow fruit," says Steve Ela. During the early years, they, too, were on the front lines in the battle with the codling moth. Their family utilized the chemical methods that were effective at the time:

Mom remembers a team of (voice command) horses pulling an orchard sprayer when they would spray lead arsenic for codling moth…And lead arsenic…They had to run [fruit] through hydrochloric acid bath afterwards to get it off…It almost makes DDT look user friendly—if you think of the time when DDT came along, of course it was a Godsend…Who wouldn't be excited about that. Later on we learned what the downstream effects are, but it's very easy to put yourself in their shoes—[DDT] was a slam-dunk.[164]

Over the years, the Elas were among other Western Slope Coloradoans who moved away from "the DDT and Tang® manufactured food era," as Ela explains it, "toward a softer program." The transition was a learning experience with many trials and errors. "It's not a quick fix. It's broader with multiple little fixes," he says, adding that it then encourages growers to plan for the long term. "We learn about the ecosystem by being organic…the system works really well if we don't screw it up. We have to control certain insects like codling moths—that's where it doesn't work," says Ela. "But we don't really need to release many [beneficial] insects if we do a good job of conserving them. They're already here."

Throughout both valleys, orchardists and viticulturists improved management strategies that aid cleaner growing: irrigation with more consistent and better drainage; installation of efficient watering systems; field management of debris, thinning and fertility; targeted weed control through mowing and digging; use of cover crops for soil health and filtration. While still vulnerable to severe winter temperatures and spring frosts, the semiarid climate is another ally of chemically cleaner fields. The Pest Management/ Control segment of the *Colorado Grape Grower Guide* discusses conditions: "The warmer and wetter the climate, the more numerous and severe disease problems are likely to be for grape growers."[165] Peaches are no exception. The National Sustainable Agriculture Information Service publication documents that as of 2012 "there is virtually no significant commercial-scale organic peach production in the East."[166]

Even farmers of non-certified organic lands on the fruit mesas and semiarid valleys of the North Fork and Grand Valley who use modern, "friendlier" sprays have had seasons where they didn't have to spray for pests at all. The amalgamation of the Western Slope's climate and eco-friendly management reached a further tipping point toward organic production in the 1990s. The passing of food production and protection laws culminated in the USDA organic program that defines "food grown and processed using no synthetic fertilizers or pesticides" as "organically grown."

Organic farming in Colorado, however, is not the "free love era" image of sandal-wearing stoner hippies who live in isolated communes. Although yes—Chaco sandals' original headquarters were in Paonia. Yes—Woodstock icon the late Joe Cocker was a longtime Crawford local. And yes—marijuana is now legal, but that is a whole other story with its own evolving history. The organic movement is big business run by highly educated growers with master's degrees in a variety of specialties like soil science, who are motivated to serve up sustainability.

Jeff Schwartz does the heavy lifting at Big B's Fabulous Juices warehouse. *Author photo.*

Western Slope operations like Aloha Organic Fruit, Delicious Orchards, Ela Family Farms and many others are part of a larger community that is "one of the fastest growing sectors of U.S. agriculture," with realized annual increases up to 20 percent since 1990.[167] As of 2012, Delta and Mesa Counties had a collective thirty-nine organic farms.[168] Colorado ranked first nationally in total organic acreage and seventh in organic fruit.[169] Overall, Colorado is a leader in organic production and considered "an emerging powerhouse" by industry experts, "contributing an estimated $2.5 billion in organic sales, or approximately 10 percent of overall U.S. sales of organic products." And the list of national and international distributors in Colorado is expanding. Yet, with limitations on irrigable land, the Western Slope will never have the larger-scale fruit industry of a Washington or a California: compare 2012 USDA census "Land in Orchards" in just one Washington State county—Yakima—at 87,607 acres versus 6,338 for the entire state of Colorado.[170]

While they might not be quantitative leaders, growers on the Western Slope are plowing an eco-friendly path—certified and non-labeled. Nonprofit organizations like the Valley Organic Growers Association (VOGA) in the North Fork Valley founded in 1992 and Slow Food Western Slope support providers and consumers of sustainable farming and clean agricultural products. Slow Food Western Slope and organic North Fork "big apple" Delicious Orchards near Paonia are not only stewards of local fare, they are all about the community table—a table that goes beyond what is on it and where it came from to who is around it. Jeff Schwartz, co-owner of Delicious Orchards, presses the idea even further, saying that they "produce food inspired by the customers."

BEE-UTIFUL

The buzzing in orchards and vineyards is not just about organics and advancements in crop management. It is from the queen of the field and her subjects. This beneficial insect has been humming through the fields of Colorado since 1862. A team of oxen led by Isaac McBroom brought in the state's first bee colony. The bees came as pollinators and producers, generating a bigger than average store of honey their inaugural year.[171] Even though this colony did not survive the winter, beekeepers were encouraged to try again.

When the Colorado State Beekeepers Association ("Bee-Keepers" at that time) incorporated in 1888, it had "the largest membership of any similar organization in the United States" with an estimated 250 colonies throughout the state. Eleven years later, the association reported (an unverified) 70,000 colonies.[172] In 1902, the industry was thrumming in the western counties with 5,000 stands, or pallets, in Delta County and 6,500 in Mesa County.[173] Frank H. Drexel writes of the early years of apiculture in Delta County for the state association's 1902 souvenir publication *Bees in Colorado*. He chronicles local and emigrant beekeepers from New York, Virginia and the Front Range, as well as his own apiarist pursuits:

> *By this time (1893) bees were in the possession of nearly every ranchman, but declining prices in honey and the panicky times brought to an untimely end many high hopes…It was at this stage that the writer, having come to this country from Baltimore in 1892 at the age of twenty-three years, for his health, entered the field of apiculture…Eight years of bee-keeping has not brought all the success dreamed of in the start, but it has brought health, has made possible the establishment of a home and a nice, clean business; the fifty colonies in one yard have grown to some four hundred, in four yards; and there is no doubt that in more competent hands the results would have been much better in many ways. All things considered, I have never felt the least regret in making Delta County my home or bee-keeping my business.*[174]

Delta and Mesa Counties were exporting around forty train carloads of honey annually during the 1920s, an abundance begotten of the Western Slope's 50 percent plus of the state's bee colonies.[175] Bees, however, are in the business of pollen production—that's where the real value is to the fruit industry…and to the bees. The honeybee is an essential pollen carrier. Fortunately for orchardists, fruit trees are one of their favorite Colorado flower sources, although not all trees need pollination. Sour cherries, most peaches and many nectarines are self-fruitful, meaning in horticulture terms they "set fruit with their own pollen."[176]

Most all fruit farmers have hives to aid in propagation, though there is no quantitative data. Not inclusive of all the small to midsize beekeeping efforts, according to the 2012 Colorado USDA reports, there are thirty-seven honey-producing farms with colonies in Delta County and forty in Mesa County. Southwestern counties of Montezuma and Montrose have twenty each. Mesa's eastern neighbor, Garfield County, has fewer farms but is ranked second highest in pounds of honey collected and comes primarily from alfalfa. While there were orchards near the turn of the century, it is now home to Blaine Colton's Epicurious Honey, a honey processor that works with Colorado-area beekeepers. Colton not only processes their honey but also extracts the pollen. Pollen demand has been increasing among those in the alternative health industry, who declare it has protein-rich benefits.

As for the health of the bees and the honey industry, that is a little sticky. In 2014, the Colorado State Beekeepers Association and the *Denver Post* reported on a Colorado State University test that found an Africanized bee in Palisade. The whole hive was destroyed to safeguard against any infestation of this tropical aggressor.[177] Pesticides and insecticides, especially the "neonicotinoids" that affect the nervous systems and cause "sub-lethal" damage, are known to cause the collapse of entire colonies.[178] Scientists have also found that a reduction in wild flower habitats is reducing wild bee populations.[179] To help determine colony health, the Western Sustainable Agriculture Research and Education Program recently funded a queen study. The project will monitor apiary and test virgin and breeder queens for disease and winter-weather resistance, as well as build up (increasing the brood) and honey production.[180]

The Colorado State Beekeepers Association has connected information like the project to beekeepers since 1880. Historically, it has fostered the apiarian culture by providing education and research. In recent years, with the advent of digital technology, it provides multiple resource avenues, with recommendations on pesticides and pests, including information on verroa mites and diseases like foulbrood. The state association has also provided advice on a furry predator with a storybook hunger for honey: the bear.

Stories of bears drawn to honey are legendary. So naturally, beekeepers discuss bear-proofing strategies to protect their hives, because when fruit is ripe and bears are loading up on calories for their winter naps, orchards in the higher mesas of North Fork County provide a smorgasbord of snacks. Holy Terror Farm outside of Paonia relies on their loyal Akbash guardian dog to protect their livestock and orchards from mesa marauders that include bears, mountain lions, deer and the ever-skillful raccoon. At Aloha Organic Orchards in Palisade, Steve Sherer's rescued lab-mix Chance is his go-to canine. "I bought him from a woman who had him chained in a culvert," says Sherer of his sidekick. "He stays on the property and chases off the deer." High Country Orchards on East Orchard Mesa above Palisade has employed an old-school wildlife deterrent that protect their peach trees from the deer: they hang bars of scented soap from the lower limbs. For others,

Canyon Wind Cellars' tasting room near the Colorado River in Paonia is a popular stopping point for people exploring the town. *Author photo.*

fencing is the only option for deer…and electric fencing for bears with a taste for port.

Canyon Wind Cellars' vineyards line up along the foot of the Grand Mesa above the Colorado River in Palisade. Their port grapes stay on the vine late into the fall to concentrate their juices. Between the winery's proximity to the national forest lands of the Grand Mesa and the rumbling bellies of pre-hibernation residents, a little nip of port berry is too good to resist. Before they were "cut off," the vineyards were their tasting room.

7

NATURAL INSPIRATION

[Art] *is symbolic—it's the earth creating also.*
—*Kay Anglim Crane, Blue Pig Gallery, 2014*

Agricultural art has been a source of historical documentation, fruit marketing strategy and heritage preservation from the beginning of habitation in Western Colorado to twenty-first-century agritourism.

Predating art galleries with classical music and wine tastings in Western Colorado, early inhabitants illustrated their history of agriculture in rock. W.C. McKern's *Western Colorado Petroglyphs* study written in 1924, but not published until discovered in the Smithsonian's National Anthropological Archives in 1977, found that the "symbols" etched into the stones were more than decorative— they included motifs of agricultural activities and milieus of early native cultivators.[181] There are thousands of petroglyphs on public Bureau of Land Management parcels in Western Colorado. These illustrations by ancient

Early agricultural rock art techniques consisted of pecking, drilling, scratching and grooving. The pecking method created a picture by dotting the surface, a prehistoric pixilation technique. Archeologists speculate natives used a variety of hollow tools for drilling, such as ones crafted from a bird's wing bone.

Even wind machines are mediums for artistic and cultural expression, as well as brand identity. *Author photo.*

and historic civilizations are more than art in agriculture. They are outdoor walls of the past.

Indoor—and outdoor—galleries in the North Fork and Grand Valleys are filled with artistic interpretations of local fruit, wine and western culture. Back roads and byways are platforms for artists who find inspiration in their pastoral and cultural surroundings. Felled orchard trees find new life as sculptures in the eyes of the Western Slope's creative community. Even the fronts and sides of buildings and barns are adorned with heritage markers, squares of Americana: quilt patterns.

BLANKETING THE BARN

Blocked, stuffed and stitched pictures of practicality covered the laps of midwestern pioneers, who passed the long, quiet hours of winter quilting.

Above: Peach trees blooming in spring at High Country Orchards. *Photo courtesy High Country Orchards & Vineyards.*

Left: Carol Zadronzny and her Z's Orchard's historical truck are both part of the Grand Valley fruit community as part of events, parades and farmers' markets. *Author photo.*

Above: Mount Garfield is the crowned promontory of the Book Cliffs across from Palisade orchards at the eastern head of the Grand Valley. *Author photo*.

Opposite, bottom left: Canyon Wind Cellars' owner/ winemaker Jennifer Christianson retired her days as a ski racing fundraiser and an environmental chemist to spend them crafting wines for their celebrated Anemoi Wine label. *Photo courtesy Canyon Wind Cellars.*

Opposite, bottom right: Aloha Organic Orchards owner/ grower Steven Sherer leads groups on agritours through his organic peach orchard in Palisade, where visitors learn how he manages the orchards and how the fruit is grown, irrigated and packed. *Author photo.*

Right: Lavender is a thriving new crop in Western Colorado, with u-pick fields like the one at Lamborn Mountain Farmstead (pictured) blooming in July. *Author photo.*

Left: Haystack Mountain cheese founder James Schott demonstrates lavender distillation to visitors at Lamborn Mountain Farmstead in Paonia during the 2014 Lavender Festival's self-guided tour. *Author photo.*

Below: Feast in the Fields at Z's Orchard (pictured) and other farm hosts, including SunCrest in 2014, is a fundraising tradition for the Palisade Chamber during the Peach Festival. *Author photo.*

Right: Colorado Mountain Winefest grape stompers go barefoot in the barrels—an event favorite on a hot September day. *Author photo.*

Below: Cyclists Michele Diamond and Sumner Schachter take a break from pedaling to celebrate Garvin Mesa Day in the West Elks AVA at Azura Cellars & Gallery. *Author photo.*

Above: Over fifty Colorado wineries, including Meadery of the Rockies (pictured), participated in the 2014 Colorado Mountain Winefest at Palisade's Riverbend Park. *Photo by Casey Hess.*

Left: The third annual Hard Cider Festival at Delicious Orchards near Paonia in 2014 featured music, beverages, BBQ, brewing demos and, of course, apples. *Author photo.*

Above: CWIDB's Doug Caskey presents the history of Colorado wine at a free seminar at the 2014 Colorado Mountain Winefest in Palisade. *Author photo*.

Right: Wine tasting in the courtyard at Azura Cellars & Gallery on Garvin Mesa, Paonia, is paired with mountain views. *Author photo*.

Opposite, top: Vineyards lining the Palisade Fruit & Wine Byway are an irrigated contrast to the rocky Western landscape. *Photo by Casey Hess*.

Opposite, bottom: Colorado's intense August sunshine is essential for concentrating the sugars for wine grapes basking on the vine. *Author photo*.

Right: Harvested grape bounty at Canyon Wind Cellars in Palisade. *Photo courtesy Canyon Wind Cellars*.

Below: Scott and Theresa High take a moment to enjoy the Colorado River setting at High Country Orchards & Vineyards. *Photo by Michael Rosacci; courtesy High Country Orchards & Vineyards*.

Above: Colorado River in DeBeque Canyon east of the Grand Valley. *Author photo*.

Left: A more efficient irrigation system is one of the changes at Clark Family Orchards from the time when Dennis Clark's (pictured) ancestors began fruit farming in Palisade in the late 1800s. *Author photo*.

Above: Workers climbing up and down ladders while pruning and picking peaches inspired artist Gary L. Hawschultz to sculpt *Pie in the Sky*. Temporarily displayed at Z's Orchard for Feast in the Field in 2014, Hawschultz's picker reaches for a single remaining peach. *Author photo*.

Right: Skilled laborers are vital to Big B's Fabulous Juices in Hotchkiss. Here they run a machine that transports organic apples to and through a filtering cider press. Juice is pumped out through a filter, and pulp is repurposed for uses like compost. *Author photo*.

Above: Canyon Wind Cellars' owner/winemaker Jay Christianson extracts wine from the barrel with a "thief" to check its fermentation. *Photo courtesy Canyon Wind Cellars.*

Left: Owner/winemaker Glenn Foster checks the Gai 2500 series line on mead bottling day. The Gai can bottle—cork, capsule or screwcap—three thousand gallons a day. *Photo courtesy Talon Wine Brands.*

Right: The Palisade Fruit & Wine Byway is a gallery of roadside art like Steve Kenty's *The Working Hand*. *Author photo.*

Below: Matthew High runs the French-engineered high-tech packing line at High Country Orchards that he says works a little like "Santa's Workshop." *Photo by William Woody; courtesy High Country Orchards & Vineyards.*

Colorado Cellars' owner/winemaker Rick Turley shows how the vintage wooden press basket operated. *Author photo.*

Besides selling fruit and vegetables, DeVries Farm Market roasts chili peppers at Glenwood Springs' Saturday Farmers' Market in autumn. Think salsa and chili relleños! *Author photo.*

Colorado Territorial Daughter and Cross Orchards Living History Farm volunteer Anamae Richmond celebrates the last jar of apple butter made during the 2009 season. Dressed in era garb, she cooks the butter on an antique stove in the renovated bunkhouse. *Photo courtesy Cross Orchards Historical Site.*

Western Slope seasonal markets like Mt. Garfield Fruit and Vegetable Stand in Clifton overflow with freshness during harvest season. *Author Photo.*

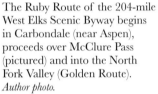

The Ruby Route of the 204-mile West Elks Scenic Byway begins in Carbondale (near Aspen), proceeds over McClure Pass (pictured) and into the North Fork Valley (Golden Route). *Author photo.*

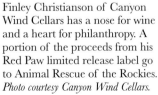

Finley Christianson of Canyon Wind Cellars has a nose for wine and a heart for philanthropy. A portion of the proceeds from his Red Paw limited release label go to Animal Rescue of the Rockies. *Photo courtesy Canyon Wind Cellars.*

Z's Orchard's barn quilt is a tribute to regional heritage. *Author photo.*

American quilt culture was born out of necessity with needle and thread and patchworks of cloth. They were utilitarian showpieces hung over drafty doors, spread over bridal beds and packed into trunks for the journey west.[182] During WWI, they were symbols of patriotism, inspired by the government's plea to "Make Quilts—Save the Blankets for our Boys over There."[183] Quilting has evolved from utilitarian craft to appliquéd heirlooms and awareness advocacy keepsakes. This art has a long history as a serviceable storyteller of life in Colorado agriculture—one that has found its way to the sides of barns, sheds and the Museum of Western Colorado.

Rather than an artist's creation of needle and thread, barn quilts are wood or metal squares painted with a pattern and hung on building exteriors. These works of art are a cultural reflection of the area or an individual property owner. They are part of a larger, growing Barn Quilt Trail that Donna Sue Groves began in Ohio to honor her heritage. Grand Valley growers and quilters who have put up this art form include local quilter "Verda," whose personal mission is "creating treasured heirlooms."

After reading an article in a 2011 issue of *Country* on Groves's trail, Verda decided to bring the idea to the Western Slope. She met with area historians and offered to make one for Cross Orchards Historical Site. After researching pattern names in a quilt encyclopedia, Verda settled on a pattern named "The Colorado Block." The quilt went up in 2012, and she followed up with two more—"Quilt of the Century," displayed at the Museum of Western Colorado in Grand Junction, and a shooting star block called "A Century of Progress." She designed the starred square for her friend Suzanne Daniels, whose son was in the military.[184]

Verda worked with a carpenter, who built eight-foot wooden squares. She taped off the patterns for clean lines and covered it using exterior base coat and semi-gloss house paint. Building quilts are subject to wear and tear, although from weather rather than washing. "The paint on the seam of the museum's quilt is flaking," Verda says. "It needs mending."

Grand Valley barn quilts are part of an undocumented trail that connects the passersby with local heritage. In addition to Verda's projects, they adorn the exterior of buildings in Western Colorado, including Z's Orchard, Kokopelli Farm Market, Dreamcatcher B&B and Cloud Terrace Farm.

CRATING ART

"Agri-lithography" is a form of art used by commercial growers back when they shipped their fruit in wooden crates and barrels. Growers separated themselves—and the products inside—from each other with fruit labels on the sides of the otherwise generic hammered and nailed boxes. The art created a visually dynamic brand identity with designs that incorporated geography, history, produce, wildlife and agricultural images.

In addition to large operations, many smaller growers and individual co-op sheds had a label. "Salesmen came around with blanks," Hotchkiss-Crawford Historical Museum volunteer Marilyn Bruce Tate says. "You could put what you wanted on it." Although many growers and packing sheds had their own brands, she adds that not everyone had a label. Even though her father did not have one when she was growing up, Marilyn took a special interest in the North Fork Valley's historical agri-lithographic art. She has archived an extensive collection of labels in a binder at the museum. Among the area's iconic labels are Union Fruit Company's Paonia Mountain Apples and the Hotchkiss Trading and Supply Company's Grizzly Brand.[185]

Priscilla Bowman Walker of the Palisade Historical Society highlights its collection of more than sixty brands in a video slideshow for center visitors. One of the most recognizable labels and one whose face varied through the years is the Mountain Lion, first used by the Grand Junction Fruit Growers' Association and later by the Cooperative Producers Association, who changed the name to Mountain Lion Fruit, Inc. in the '60s.

Brand recognition logos on pre-printed cardboard containers eventually replaced fruit labels pasted to the side of wooden crates. Pre-printed label supplies that went unused found new purpose and evolved beyond images traveling the world stuck on the side of a plank inside a dark railcar. During the days of meager living, when being thrifty was not a choice, farmers patched walls and ceilings with extra labels. Labels are now vintage art—framed and hung in museums and domestic kitchens or replicated in museum notecards and Smithsonian calendars.

A modern generation of Western Slope growers carries the tradition of label art forward. Delicious Orchards and their Big B's Hard Cider product art was inspired by early fruit labels from the North Fork area like the Grizzly Brand in Hotchkiss. Palisade's High Country Orchards label redesign is a dynamic melding of vintage art with graphic design. "Our vision was to have it look like the labels of one hundred years ago," says Theresa High, adding that it needed to fit today's packaging requirements while still

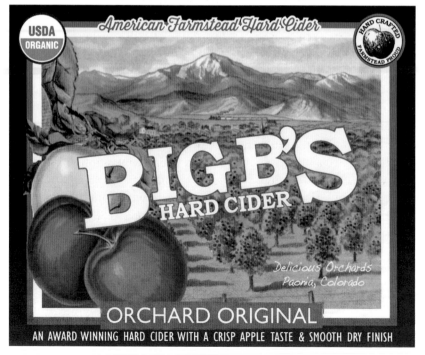

being nostalgic. High and her husband, Scott, took their ideas to Colorado artists. A watercolor artist painted a rendering of High's "perky peach" that served as a template for a team of graphic designers, who came up with the final product after several rounds of tweaking.[186] After all, good art—like wine—takes time to develop. High says the same artist who worked on the label helped design the Palisade Fruit & Wine Byway signage that steers agritourists through to the growers on the confusing maze of county roads.

When tourists stop along Palisade's byway at the High Country Orchards & Vineyards tasting room, they also get a sampling of Scott High's vision for a sculpture garden with the first piece of his corkscrew museum project. The red ball in the corkscrew piece has its own history: a harbor mine used during WWII and later used as a San Francisco Bay buoy. There's even a big black ball and chain sculpture—the chain coming from a 1940s naval ship—that was a birthday gift to Theresa. She used to joke, "This orchard is my ball and chain. None of what we've done has come easily." She says all the sculptures have meaning. "That big peach out there," High, mother of three, says, "*James and the Giant Peach* was one of Keenan's favorite books."

A LOVELY COMPLEMENT

"Making wine and art is creatively similar," says Ty Gillespie of Azura Cellars. "You're making something from scratch. In both cases, your imagination produces the outcome for art or wine."

Gillespie and his wife, Helen, are artists who used to run a farmers' market near Vail. Deciding they wanted to be closer to the growing region, they explored Delta County's North Fork Valley. "We started driving around up in the hills and found this wonderful piece of land," says Gillespie. They settled on the Garvin Mesa property above Paonia with the intention of starting an art gallery, but since the mesa was home to wineries, they found a mentor in local enologist guru Steve Rhodes and began winemaking. Gillespie adds that their gallery and wine-tasting offering is "a good example" of art and enology's natural pairing. "The customers are mutual."

Opposite, top: Fruit crate labels like the Grizzly Brand are now collectables. *Palisade Historical Society photo; courtesy of Hugh Coachman.*

Opposite, bottom: Big B's label is inspired by the historic Grizzly Brand label. *Author photo, label art courtesy of Delicious Orchards.*

Artists like the Gillespies seem to be drawn to the area. Through the efforts of this community's active visual, performance and agrarian artists, the North Fork Valley became a Colorado Certified Creative District in 2013. Certification came out of Colorado legislative bill HB11-1031, enacted to encourage artistic entrepreneurs to develop, promote and celebrate community diversity and quality.[187] North Fork Valley's artistic communities go beyond the awards of certification. Backyard studios, town park events and historic centers throughout Delta County spotlight the creative culture—often in a historic setting.

The AppleShed in Cedaredge on the south slope of the Grand Mesa houses fine and décor art under the repurposed roof of an old packing shed. It, too, combines the visual palate with epicurean tastes. In AppleShed's case, that includes wine, cider and pie. A 1939 creamery building in Hotchkiss is now an art center with a gallery showcasing over fifty local artists, education programs for all ages, a Saturday farmers' market and, of course, ice cream. Home for Blue Sage Center for the Arts in Paonia is in two notable buildings, one of which is on the Colorado Register of Historic Places. The Blue Sage Center has celebrated and featured the eclectic nature of North Fork art for over twenty years, providing a venue for exhibits and events, as well as collaboration on community activities.

Similar to the Blue Sage in Paonia, Palisade's Blue Pig Gallery is a celebration of local creativity. Both have an appeal beyond their zip code, and the Blue Pig has garnered a reputation as a destination gallery. "We're well known and respected enough that people come from miles around to visit us," says director and artist Kay Crane. She adds, "People who are traveling through like to take back a piece of the Grand Valley."

Contests throughout the state have become showcases for agriculture-inspired art. The Colorado Farm Fresh Guide sent out a call for submissions for their thirtieth anniversary issue in 2014, choosing graphic artist Nanci Avery's colorful tableau for the directory's cover. The state also sponsors the photography contest, *Colorado…it's AgriCultural*, a visual celebration of agrarian heritage. The Colorado Association for Viticulture and Enology, CAVE, holds an annual statewide contest for original art to represent its events. Crane won it in 2014. She says she thought about the idea for a long time. Her inspiration came from the surrounding landscape, not competition:

> *Artists are here to create. We think about it all the time. There is the beauty of nature everywhere, but there is a particular appeal to agriculture—the rows of orchards and vineyards. I'm struck when I go by how beautiful their patterns are.*[188]

"Vineyard View" by Kay Crane

The 2014 Colorado Winefest poster is from Kay Crane's winning art submission, "Vineyard View." *Photo courtesy CAVE.*

ART-IN-FACT

There is also an art to preserving agricultural history. The Hotchkiss-Crawford Historical Museum is full of photographs that show the cultivation of North Fork Valley. Delta became the "City of Murals" after an urban renewal project in the 1980s that transformed buildings into canvased tours of bygone days. The Palisade Historical Society's window is a framed display of creations from the Grand Valley's past. And the Cross Orchard Historical Site in Grand Junction is a living showcase of fruit culture's early years: antique trucks and machinery lined up in the yard became metal sculptures, monuments to those who spent their days behind the wheels; the old packing shed walls feature peach picking sacks and pruning stilts. There's a spinning wheel, paintings, quilts and tools that add to a collective exhibit of inventions and handiwork—artifacts that tell fourth graders and other school groups the story of agricultural life in the Grand Valley.

The Cross Orchards site also began Two Rivers Chautauqua two-day productions in 2006, featuring theatric performances by historic characters. Kit Carson, Teddy Roosevelt, Otto Mears—reincarnates of

An evolution of peach-picking sacks, an invention born of an apron, displayed at Cross Orchards Historical Site. *Author photo.*

Much of the vintage machinery displayed at Cross Orchards Historical Site comes from area farms. *Author photo.*

figures who shaped Western Colorado's fruit and wine future—bring their stories to the present.

Director Kay Fiegel says that another of Cross Orchards' events, Fall Day on the Farm, draws up to 1,200 people. "Agriculture has played a major role in the development of this valley," Fiegel says. "Somebody's got to tell its story." Cross Orchards isn't the only one relaying this narrative among the various art forms. Fiegel describes how "generations come to come together," on Fall Day. Grandparents share "their personal heritage during the day talking and walking down their memory lanes."[189] This art form is an invisible thread that draws ages together.

8
SUSTAINABLE SUCCESSION

See, a sprout is like a teenager.
—*Harry Talbott, Talbott's Mountain Gold, 2014*

The North Fork Heart & Soul Project—an Orton Family Foundation model—has a Vision 2020 plan for the future that values established heritage and adapts to evolving traditions. Vision 2020 is a collective view from over 1,300 valley residents, who, through Pass the Mic interviews, Slice of the Pie focus groups and other forums, shared their views on the future. A steady economy was one of the five values they identified. Solution ideas included two actions: "Create a sustainable food and wine sector," and "Get young people interested in agriculture."[190]

Although the conversations were from the North Fork community, the culture in the Grand Valley is similar. Fruit and wine are primary economic contributors in both regions, and a 2012 USDA census reported principal operator age average in Delta and Mesa Counties is fifty-nine. As a demographic, rural youth are migrating to urban lifestyles.

In spite of statistics and trends, however, there is a minority of young people who are sowing a future in Western Slope fruit-lands. They are new contributors to old heritage.

IT'S GENERATIONAL

Dennis Clark was a young man when he left the family orchard business to study accounting at college. Then after his parents expanded the fruit farm to over fifty acres, he "just started coming back." Soon Clark was back full time and has been there ever since. He says his daughters have an interest in the business, especially his oldest, a recent CSU graduate. Clark hopes she takes some time, explores a little and makes sure that she wants to come back to a fruit-growing career.[191]

Steve Ela says he also went "off to college," earned a master's degree in soil science and "did other things." Ela gave "coming back" to their farm in the North Fork Valley a lot of thought. "I knew once I made that decision…" He paused. "It's a big decision. My chosen profession—it's hard, really hard work." Will his kids continue Ela Family Farms into a fifth generation? His eleven-year-old already talks about it. No pressure, says Dad. "It can happen if they want it to."[192]

Two of Harry Talbott's four sons, Charlie and Bruce, left Palisade to travel the world. They worked apple orchard crops in Cornwall, England. They picked wine grapes in Normandy, France. They went to Spain and harvested citrus. The brothers went to Greece, Israel and Bangkok. After the better part of two years, they parted directions. Bruce went on to Hong Kong, and Charlie became an Australian cowboy down under. Both came back to Palisade. Both are partners in Talbott Farms.[193] Charlie Talbott thinks it's good for youth to see what's beyond their family roots. "It's best to come back with a different set of perspectives, having cross-pollinated. With that fresh set of eyes, you don't wonder, 'what did I leave on the table?'"[194]

Clarks, Elas, Talbotts—each of these fourth- and fifth-generation fruit farmers has built ownership equity on the foundation of their ancestors. Clark, Ela and the Talbott siblings, Charlie and Bruce—and their brother, Nathan—have all raised a new generation that may or may not succeed them in their businesses. Nathan Talbott says he sees how much pride his father takes in watching his sons grow the business. He hopes one day he'll have that same vantage point with his own children, adding that their company was designed to be multi-generational. Charlie Talbott sums it up: "What we have here is a small industry, but we have a legacy."[195] It is a legacy they did not want to languish, so they created a succession strategy that provides a map for the future. Their plan includes a personal buy-in with the purchase of land that the business operates through a lease basis and with the buyer

Bruce and son Harry Charles (circa 1995) are fifth- and sixth-generation Talbott Palisade fruit farmers. *Photo courtesy Talbott Farms.*

working on a career basis. The idea is adding to, not pulling from, the equity. Charlie Talbott shares the notion:

> *When the day comes and you don't want to be doing this anymore you have two choices. The business continues beyond you intact or you sell.* [With a succession plan] *the hope and the expectation is they continue to grow the business…help take it to the next level…The mechanism for compensation at some point will include partnership interest…It's a grand scheme full of hope and opportunity. It's exciting.*

In 2014, a sixth generation of Talbotts decided to join the family business, becoming part of Palisade's fruit-grower community. Harry "Charles" Talbott V joined his father, uncles and grandfather in the business—although not until after he first left the valley, coming back after service in the U.S. Marine Corps.

TRUST IN THE FUTURE

During a ten-year period (1997–2007), Mesa County averaged a loss of twenty-five and a half orchard acres per year, with an annual economic hit of $280,000.[196]

Even with a potential infusion of youth into fruit farming on the Western Slope, it is not sustainable without affordable acreage. The Mesa Land Trust was one of the first in the country to protect farmland from development. The Black Canyon Regional Land Trust (BCRLT) collaborative effort began the following decade in the North Fork of the Gunnison and Uncompahgre Watershed areas.

Generally, farmers donate their development property rights to these conservation trusts, ensuring a perpetual agrarian use regardless of energy booms or encroaching urbanization that drive up land costs. In turn, this designated farm acreage is used, leased or sold according to a more affordable agricultural market value. This was an additional reason Charles Talbott V was able to continue a multigenerational tradition—he bought property in 2014 that was under a conservation easement.[197]

Trusts make the farm lifestyle an accessible investment choice for a younger demographic. Leasing easements also help, providing a link between those without succession heirs and families without start-up capital. That is the story of Blakely and Mike Mechau of Palisade, who, when they retired, leased their land to the Washkowiaks. The Washkowiak family put their expertise to work and started growing organic produce. Their Field to Fork CSA bounty is now shared with one hundred families and is served at restaurant tables throughout Mesa County, including BIN 707 Foodbar, il Bistro Italiano and No Coast Sushi. The opportunity provided to them by the Mechaus and the Mesa Land Trust has enabled the Washkowiaks' business to grow enough so they could purchase their own land—a farm next to their agricultural allies, friends and now neighbors, the Mechaus.[198]

To date, the BCRLT protects fifty thousand acres and the Mesa Land Trust more than sixty-four thousand, with Mesa reporting that in a five-year span, they conserved ten dollars in land value for every one dollar spent on operating costs.

Agriculture's newest demographic is not only aided by conservation trusts and seasoned mentors, they are banding together to help each other. The mission of the National Young Farmers Coalition, founded by three

East Coast Hudson Valley visionaries, is to "work in coalition with farmers, consumers, organizations and government to tackle the many challenges that young, independent and sustainable farmers face in their first years of operating a farm business." Kate Greenberg is their Western Slope Organizer, and Beginning Farmers and Ranchers of Mesa County is the Western Slope chapter affiliate.[199]

Even with this youthful energy, sustaining an industry does not only fall onto the shoulders of those driving tractors, pulling weeds and mobilizing support. It comes from crop diversification—something that early fruit farmers learned when Fruita's apple business rotted, Elberta peaches ripened at the same time and frost killed off crops that might not have been well suited for the multiple Western Slope microclimates. The need for diversification is one of the primary reasons peach growers planted grapes in the 1970s. In the new millennium, enter lavender and hops.

The Lavender Association of Western Colorado organized in 2009 around a new cash crop potential that thrives under the plentiful sunshine. What began as a small group has evolved into a movement with forty-eight member growers. Supported by the CSU Extension–Tri-River Area, the association provides lavender-growing enthusiasts with research, guidance

Wind machines of various ages tower above the crops, where at one time only smudge pots and fires helped to protect new growth. *Author photo.*

The lifespan of peach trees has shortened over time due to many environmental factors. Growers looking toward the future planted thousands of new trees in 2015. *Author photo.*

and facts on propagating, harvesting and distilling. Their July festival invites the public to learn about the fragrant crop during three days of tours, seminars and demonstrations. Of course, fans of the spiked flower don't just include aromatherapists, chefs and crafters. It's possible that none could be more pleased with the budding industry than the bees.

As for hops, where there's beer, there's a hop market. The Colorado Department of Agriculture boasts its home turf as the largest beer-producing state in the country.[200] Nationally, they rank third in craft breweries, with only 5 percent of the hops grown in state.[201] A 2012 *Draft* magazine article referenced Colorado Hop Grower Association's agronomist guru Ron Godin as saying that members sold all their harvest in less than two months.[202] Statistics from 2014 by the Hop Growers of America show that Colorado strings an estimated seventy-five acres of hops. Interest in raising the flowering cone is expanding and not even close to a foamy head yet.

Next up for those old enough to belly up to the bar: distilleries. Colorado Distillers Guild's Rob Masters writes how

Colorado distillers are taking old-world traditions and making new variations using locally sourced raw goods that impart Colorado terroir. Vodka using Colorado honey (Spring44)…and brandy (Peach Street Distillers, Peak Spirits) from fruit grown in Colorado's Western Slope

orchards…In order to make world-class spirits, you need to start with world-class ingredients.[203]

SEEDLING PROJECTS

The issuing of property and traditions is also sorted, labeled, packaged and checked out with a library card. "Seeds contain stories, recipes and a way of life that is passed from one gardener to the next," writes the North Fork Seed Library in Hotchkiss. Its heirloom seed library began with a mini-grant from the Heart & Soul Project, seed donations from companies and community members and long hours of organization by staff and volunteers. Heirloom seed planting ranges from easy to advanced to ensure no cross-pollination adulteration. Unlike hybrids, heirloom varieties are old cultivars that regenerate year after year, as long as seeds are saved and reused. While gardeners can check out seeds, they don't have to return them. They can, however, donate them along with a narrative on their growing history and photos of the process. It's North Fork Seed Library's vision that seed saving "inspires a sense of heritage and a community of giving."

Giving back to the North Fork community has been heaped high on plates of spaghetti and served up by the Kids' Pasta Project (KPP) since 2009. KPP youth serve the community—literally—at fundraising dinners and donate the profits to local causes. KPP chefs create culinary philanthropy using tomatoes from Thistle Whistle Farm for the marinara, meatballs made with grass-fed

Paonia's few downtown blocks include the Blue Sage Center for the Arts and the Living Farm Café—both in historical buildings. *Author photo.*

cattle from Princess Beef and Jonathan apples from Ela Family Farms for their apple crisp dessert. KPP uses local ingredients whenever possible. The project is philanthropic, collaborative and educational. Eleni's Greek Restaurant, Delicious Orchards, Fresh & Wyld Farmhouse Inn and Blue Sage Center for the Arts are past dinner venues. Partner-recipients in 2014 included Mountain Harvest Festival and Slow Food Western Slope. Kids involved in the program learn teamwork and problem solving, as well as other transferable life and job skills besides those required for a restaurant. KPP annually averages twenty dinners, requiring over four thousand volunteer hours.[204]

Some business-minded youth with a taste for growing local economies in fruit and wine country are following their passions to their own backyard. The Austin Family Farm Honey Company is the brainchild of Austin children. The "Three Abeegos"—two brothers and their cousin—started the business in 2008 at ages eleven to thirteen. Mentored and supported by adults, this new generation of beekeepers is making more than honey. They're making headlines. They won their age category (twelve to fourteen) in the 2009 Celebration for Young Entrepreneurs, a Colorado competition that recognizes the efforts of business owners under twenty-one years old.[205] The Three Abeegos are the newest members in a long line of family farming that spans two states and seven generations.

These youth and their investments in local community and business are lively exceptions to the emigration trend.

No Small Potatoes

The future of fruit-farming culture does not add up to continuance, even with succession plans, pasta, youthful ingenuity and generations of footsteps. In spite of the agricultural and ranching landscape expanse in the North Fork and Grand Valleys, most of the youth there did not grow up on a farm. Add to that the mass exodus from farm country by young Americans. Factor in a lifestyle with an unpredictable profit margin and predictable dawn to dusk sweat. What Western Slope agriculture is left with is a disconnect with those able to plant the future.

Science teacher Cassandra Shenk started Teens on Farms in hopes of impacting a change in the equation by introducing young people to farm culture.

Shenk moved to the North Fork Valley from Big Horn, Montana country and brought big ideas with her. She started Teens on Farms in

2009 as a pilot program with one primary goal: put every willing teenager to work on farms. She wanted the *text gens* to learn work ethics, based on the ideal that work generates self-worth. Her intent was to show teens that farming is a viable career choice and one that is part of the valley. "Almost everybody who was raised here has a story about packing fruit," Shenk says. "It influenced their lives."

Her study began with learning why the maturing farmers weren't tapping into the teen population for help. The study found the main reason was networking. "Older farmers didn't have connections with kids," Shenk explains, adding a sub-factor. "They didn't believe kids knew *how* to work." Peripheral reasons encompassed liability issues and financial resource limitations.

"Hyper, young" students without summer jobs were Shenk's first group to bridge the cultural gap. It began with twelve kids, and program numbers fluctuated over the years. During this time, Teens on Farms participants also launched "Plants Are Us," a garden of their own at the Delta County

Heritage tourism is a growing trend among Western Colorado historical communities like Palisade. *Author photo.*

Fairgrounds. The program has benefited from many mentors, including Scott Horner on Small Potatoes Farm. He leases the land from an elderly couple who were part of one of the success stories Shenk tells.

Shenk taught a quiet fourteen-year-old who had expressed an interest in learning to farm. She found an opportunity for him, but the farmer called after only a few days and said he wasn't working out. A second placement followed with the same end result. When Shenk asked, they said he did the work but needed constant direction, requiring time they didn't have. The student confirmed that he really did want to learn so she tried one more time with Wayne and Monica Wiitanen. A week passed with no word. She called. "There's nothing wrong with this kid," Wayne Wiitanen said in a matter-of-fact demeanor. Shenk called again later, and Monica Wiitanen answered. "Not only is he working out," she said, "the days he's here Wayne gets out of bed a littler earlier. He's a little happier."

Fast-forward two years, and the student is their greenhouse manager. He's more outgoing. There's a generational and cultural bond.

Will this youth or other Teens on Farms become the next generation of fruit farmers, ranchers, beekeepers and growers that decides the direction of Western Slope agriculture? Shenk says the idea was to expose kids to the farming lifestyle and to connect them with the established culture. She adds that even if only one out of twenty or fifty youth end up becoming a farmer, it's a success.[206]

There is a seedling of success, too, because of the experiences these and all the youth have had. They have walked the pathways laid down by row after row of fruit farmer and now have a history that can be shared at any table.

9

STEWARDS OF NOTE

The agricultural stewards of the Grand and North Fork Valleys are too numerous to honor each here. Everyone who shared their stories—and those whose voices are not echoed in these pages—is an essential contributor to the larger narrative of the Western Slope's history. The profiles that are included are really conversations, insights into the people behind the fruit baskets and wine barrels. They are a bountiful sampling of exceptional people in the valleys—a whetting of the appetite.

Included after these consumer-meet-grower introductions is a resource list, a partial directory of the abundant up-to-date fruit grower guides that list farms, events and markets. They serve as maps, featuring special stops for the agritourist, as well as a directional to historical communities for the heritage tourist. Heritage tourists are a new class of traveler who seeks a connection to the past and who are often one in the same with the agritourist. The sources provided here are by no means comprehensive. They are just a few road signs to help you on your way. Safe travels.

MEET CAROL ZADROZNY,
AKA MRS. Z.: Z'S ORCHARD

It's a Monday at Z's in late August, and there's no market. Carol is in a historical old shed, packing peaches to ship to customers all over the country.

The owners of Z's Orchard, Carol Zadrozny and Richard Skaer, planted broomcorn and sunflowers to honor their Oklahoma and Kansas ancestries. *Author photo.*

She says the peaches they ship are mostly to repeat customers for special occasions like birthdays or "just because." Carol's husband, Richard Skaer, is spending Monday indoors with his accountant hat on. Earlier in the month, he'd been outside, donning his do-what-needs-done lid. He was up on ladders, picking peaches alongside Mario Lopez, their year-round "amazing professional orchardist," who has been part of the Z family for ten years. Meanwhile, Carol's neighbor Ginger Whittington helps out at the Country Store, greeting a customer who just came in from the field with pails of u-pick raspberries. Besides neighbors, friends and family, other help around the orchard this season comes from a college intern; the 2014 Peach Queen, Bailey McCall; and two seasonal employees.

Spirited, but no spring chickens, Carol and Richard were both widows and started a new life on the property in 1972 when they retired from teaching. She says they were very fortunate to be able to buy it, due in part to an old-fashioned "farm swap": They traded their property in Grand Junction near the Colorado Monument in exchange for the Palisade orchard. "Before you knew it," says Carol, "we were peach farmers."

Back at the start, they had some drive-up business, but most of what they sold went to the co-op. When the automation kept breaking down, friends came over to help—even going so far as to contract truckers for Z's. Then the original packing shed burned down. In the 1980s, the crops "froze three years straight." After those years of frost, Carol and Richard went down to Arizona and bought a secondhand wind machine to help protect the peaches in the microclimate on her side of the "draw," a wide ditch that runs through East Orchard Mesa. Z's Orchard also branched out. They planted apples, berry bushes and flowers, put in a commercial kitchen, added handcrafted goods in their market, and brought in chickens and bees—a natural fit for their fruit and flowers. Their hive-home base is over near the ponds and gardens on C Road, from where the bees travel the rural neighborhood in up to a one-mile radius. Carol laughs, gestures in the air and says they feast on a "smorgasbord of stuff."

In spite of wind machines, pollination and diversification, the fruit harvest is unpredictable, without guaranteed yields. "Every year is different. You never know what's going to happen until they're on the tree ready to pick," Carol says. "You don't know."

Z's participation in the Peach Festival's Feast in the Field has been one constant over the past years, an event that raises funds for the Palisade Chamber of Commerce. At their 2014 orchard dinner, chefs from il Bistro Italiano in Grand Junction prepared an appetizer and four-course culinary fare using fruit, vegetables, cheeses and meats from local farms and ranches. A team of volunteers presented plates and poured Plum Creek Winery wine pairings while Richard told stories and visited with the guests. With the onset of dusk, Carol offered diners a spritz of lavender hydrosol to ward off any uninvited mosquitos.

Carol hosted the feast because it helps "people connect to the earth." What she read in Pearl S. Buck's *The Good Earth* years ago still resonates for her. "We feel blessed to have this twenty acres—to be stewards of the earth," Carols says of the lifestyle that she, Richard and their ancestors chose. She adds that it is "something that honors our heritage." She credits her parents and grandparents with the bounty in her life, a lifestyle shared by their children and grandchildren should they choose it. The alternative is for bigger growers to lease the land or to sell the family farm. For now, Carol, Richard and their many helping hands pack up the truck—except Mondays—and travel to farmers' markets throughout the Rocky Mountain states region and into Kansas.

MEET THERESA HIGH:
HIGH COUNTRY ORCHARDS & VINEYARDS

"Rootstock," Theresa High says. "It's very important that you choose the right rootstock for your fruits." The Highs are incorporating new rootstock with hearty characteristics in their older, more established Palisade farmlands. The rootstocks come to Mesa County from different parts of the country, from places like New York's Finger Lakes region. Not unlike Theresa, who is also a transplant.

She grew up on her family's forty acres, surrounded by fruit farms in Romeo, Michigan, and put down new roots in Palisade. Only in Theresa's case, the fruit chose her. She says she never planned to be in agriculture, let alone grow peaches. Becoming a peach farmer and grape grower just kind of happened, sown after college and career and by a love for travel, wine and Scott High.

Scott and Theresa High's shared passions took them all over the world before they got married. They traveled to wineries and vineyards and talked about having one of their own someday. Then along with Scott's marriage proposal came a promise: a vineyard. The question after "yes" was where. They considered the south of France, Oregon or Washington, until they thought about how much they loved Colorado. That's when they set their sights on Palisade.

Scott High—a Colorado native with viticulture training in Germany—knew that the Western Slope was a special place with favorable grape-growing conditions. So in October 1999, they bought a past-its-prime orchard from the Nicolays on East Orchard Mesa above Palisade, just off the curve in the road where E½ becomes 35½ Road. They intended to replace the old Yakima Hale peach trees with a vineyard. "That's what's going to be at the end of this rainbow," Theresa says. The peaches on the property had other ideas.

"When I came here I had no intention of [becoming a peach farmer]," she says. "I just found myself up here one April day, knowing that I had to get the [packing] building done, and we were going to pack peaches in July, and that Mother Nature was not going to wait." The peaches kept producing, and Theresa kept packing, learning along the way from Western Slope growers who shared their time and expertise, especially Bob and Sherri Nicolay, her "guardian angels." She says they didn't just sell her a piece of land. They mentored her like family, helping her carry forward a Palisade fruit-growing legacy.

What started as a part-time job for her became a full-time venture. "Before I knew it," she says, "we had sixty-five acres by 2005—no grapes yet, all peaches." Even the home site they settled on had peach trees. Finally, by the next year, they found the first of their four grape-growing properties: Katie's Vineyard, named for their daughter. Now they had the vines but not the winemaking facilities. In 2008, Two Rivers Winery & Chateau in Grand Junction bottled the Highs' first vintage under the Colterris Winery label. After two years of maturing in oak, they released it at the 2010 Colorado Mountain Winefest. Colterris wines continue to be produced and bottled at Two Rivers Winery from 100 percent High Country Orchards & Vineyards estate grown grapes, a collaborative effort of oenophiles that also includes enologist Ty Lawson and viticulturist Napa Valley industry transplant Tony Fernandez.

Over the years, their farmland has grown to 126 acres: 9,000 cherry trees, 33,881 vines, a lavender garden consisting of 165 plants of five different varieties and 32,000 peach trees. Their market for tree-ripe peaches has also expanded, thanks to the installation of a high-tech machine run by employees that carefully sizes, sorts and packs peaches in minutes. The boxes of fruit are loaded onto trucks, and within twenty-four hours, tree-ripened peaches are on store shelves: farmers' market freshness sold indoors for grocer partners like Whole Foods.

Some of those peach trees are propagated Yakima Hale heirloom clippings, descendants from the property's original orchard that still produce fruit…and Theresa's still picking it. Her mom told Theresa she has come full circle, adding, "Isn't it interesting how you've come back to your roots." Theresa hadn't really seen it while it was happening. "It wasn't until after I was here, when I started to look back at the journey my life has taken," she says. "But I found myself."

(FYI: Notre Dame fans, you can find Colterris on the virtual ND Wine Tour that lists wineries across the country operated by alumni, parents and friends of Notre Dame.)

MEET HARRY TALBOTT: TALBOTT FARMS

Octogenarian peach patriarch Harry Talbott is a storyteller—and with good reason. His family has a long, established Western Slope history that spans from Cedaredge to Eckert to Rapid Creek to Palisade. With Harry's son

Charlie helping to add flavor to the story, he begins his fruit-farming tale with the matrilineal branch of the family tree.

Harry's great-grandfather Joseph Evan Yeager migrated from Iowa around 1907. The first peaches he put up were in Rapid Creek, just above Palisade. Next came the Talbotts from Kentucky—land of the Hatfields and McCoys (they are descendants of the very same…Charlie McCoy and Mary Britten). Later, in 1930, Harry A. Talbott met Margaret P. Yeager. They parented the lineage of children (Harry), grandchildren and great-grandchildren who continue fostering Colorado's largest peach farming operation.

Harry sits at the head of the Talbott Farms table flanked by his sons over one hundred years after his ancestors first came to Colorado. "The old-timers thought life was hard," he says. But growing up, he adds, "We had lots of fun, we just did things." Plus, there was no law that said you *couldn't* ride your horse on the sidewalk in Palisade.

The 1940s brought the war years, and their independent Top of the Nation brand peaches "sold like hotcakes." When the '50s rolled in, the Talbotts diversified. Charlie says his grandfather was "very industrious and had a real knack for embracing a new business idea and making it work." One idea was starting a poultry business in the '50s that supplied eggs to City Market and King Soopers.

They had thousands of turkeys and chickens. "Egg machines," Harry calls them. "One thing about the chickens," Harry says, "is that we could always pay the people, pay our bills during the year, see…and then we had the harvest." Besides, "chicken manure is good for peaches." It was Harry's morning job to feed the chickens and pick up the dead turkeys ("they just died sometimes"). If he "drew the short straw," he had to clean the houses, too. All this pungent duty "inspired his young mind" to rationalize eating breakfast afterward for the sake of not losing it.

When Harry came of age for college, he studied at a long list of universities including Mesa State, University of California–Davis and Christian-based Ottawa University in Kansas. While on school break, he met his wife, Bonnie, at the Baron Lake church camp on the Grand Mesa. "I just decided I'm gonna marry her," Harry says. Lucky for him, she agreed. Harry and the boys may sit at the table, but she sets it. Once a week, she gathers family, friends and peers around the dinner (noontime in farm country) table. They take time out of their busy schedules to share meals and time and maybe, if Barbara Bikki of Bikki's Ranch of Liberty stops by, Hungarian stuffed cabbages. Then one by one, they say their goodbyes and disperse back to their responsibilities.

For the Talbott clan, in the new-millennium that means oversight of approximately 450 acres of owned and leased land, with thirty-two peach varieties and over twenty-four wine grapes, including viniferous and French hybrids sold to over twenty-five wineries. They also raise pears, pack fruit for other growers and press apple cider that's sold to Walmart, City Market and Kroger grocery chains. They say growth and change have been "enormous" over the years. Although as Charlie says, "We're not in the business of buying and selling land." Their mission is to "produce value from the land," and that includes protecting it from development.

Prompted by encroaching oil shale boom interests, Harry Talbott cofounded the Mesa Land Trust in 1980. Two years later, Bonnie and Harry donated one of its first conservation easements. More recently, after years of board service and program support, Harry Talbott and Talbott Farms won the 2013 Friends of the Open Space at the Fourth Annual Southern Colorado Conservation Awards. The award honors "efforts that led to the protection of a significant property or landscape in Colorado." The Talbotts are committed to sustaining the industry that has written their history. Anyone who wants to learn more about it just needs to ask Harry.

"See, I can remember stories—I got a mind like a movie camera," he says. "I can go back and rewind."

(By the way, Charlie's book recommendation is Norwegian-American author Ole Edvart Rølvaag's *Giants in the Earth*.)

Meet Joan and John Mathewson: Terror Creek Winery

Old World style, with North Fork Valley verve—that's the Mathewsons.

The Mathewsons lived, worked and traveled around the world before starting the winery (named for the property's creek that in early settlement days was a "holy terror" during run-off). They became accustomed to the European custom of wine served as a palate partner to the meal. Having a winery became part of their long-term plan. So while John, a geophysicist, was employed in North Africa, Joan apprenticed in the Canton of Valais (home of the Matterhorn), Switzerland's largest wine region. Over a five-year period of working on and off in vineyards and wineries, she gained enough experience to take a winemaker examination at *L'Ecole de Changins* (The School of Changins) in Nyon. Certificate in hand, Joan rejoined her husband.

How they got to the North Fork Valley from Nigeria is thanks to a letter from their friend and Colorado wine industry pioneer Bennett Price of DeBeque Canyon Winery. Included in the post was an article from the *Rocky Mountain News* about land (owned by three Chicagoans) near Paonia that was for sale. Elk herds and grazing cattle had stomped down the grapes. They tell how a man—Al Barbero—who came to hunt with the property's caretaker discovered the vines, abandoned the hunting intention and dedicated his time to getting them off the ground and thriving again. What was intriguing to the Mathewsons was that it was also the site of original Four Corners' plantings. "It was a good omen that the property would be fruitful," Joan says, since the "Gewurztraminer grapevines planted in the 1970s were still growing!"

The next time they came back to the States, they directed their travel through the Western Slope. The Mathewsons were new to the North Fork Valley but not strangers to Colorado. John went to the School of Mines and was a first lieutenant with the Camp Hale's Tenth Mountain Division near Leadville. Joan came from New Jersey to go to Colorado Women's College (at the University of Denver) and worked at Aspen's legendary Red Onion. They met at college and again in Aspen. Together they lived, as Joan says, "through a lot of history."

The vineyard chapter of their story began at age sixty-four when they bought the property, settling into North Fork culture and a life dedicated to winemaking. The Mathewsons established Terror Creek Winery in the early '90s. Their commercial wine operation is among the highest in the world at an elevation of 6,417 feet, with tasting room views that hint of Europe.

Some friends from Switzerland helped them plant their first acre: new Gewurztraminer alongside the old. In keeping with Joan's training, the wines they make are the primarily dry French, Alsatian-style. Their vineyard technique is meticulous. Joan says the vines need to be "properly tied up" and the vineyard trim and clean, adding how each is individual—"each plant deserves attention."

"[Starting a winery is] not the way to retire" Joan says with a soft laugh and over twenty years of proprietorship under her size-small belt, but "we've had a great time."

Meet Carol and James Schott: Lamborn Mountain Farmstead

It all began with a goat—actually, five goats.

James Schott visited a Front Range goat dairy with his youngest daughter back in the late 1980s. Around the same time, he had shelved his PhD in academia and many years in education to learn traditional French cooking at a culinary school in Wisconsin. Preparing food with goat cheese was part of the lesson plan. He came back to Colorado, bought four does and a buck, and that was the beginning of Haystack Mountain goat cheese near Boulder. As Boulder and his business grew, James—a widower—met back up with Carol, a longtime colleague in education and friend. They married in 1999 and Carol joined Haystack, where she started making soap.

With development pressure elbowing in and the corporate side of cheese taking up James's time, they set their sights over the Rocky Mountains to the North Fork Valley. They bought a 1905 house and farm with panoramic views on Lamborn Mesa in 2002 and moved over seven years later to begin their retirement activities. No, not sleeping late and playing golf. Like many who "retire" in the valley, they started a new enterprise: small-scale organic farming.

The goats (milk) followed…and Scottish Highland Cattle joined them.

Only two months after the move, Carol and James saw an ad in the newspaper announcing the first ever meeting of the Lavender Association of Western Colorado. "I got interested in lavender because I was making soap for Haystack," Carol says. "And [the] lavender was popular." They went to the meeting and connected with people who shared their interest. The next step was to begin growing lavender. The Schotts planted in the fall, lost most of the crop due to an extreme winter and replanted in the spring of 2010. Today, Lamborn has blooming fields of lavender—Dulce, Miss Katherine and other varieties. "The association," Carol says, was "very instrumental in helping us. We didn't have to do it by ourselves." After five years, the Western Slope lavender industry is still in development. "We're all still learning."

A trip to the Lamborn Mountain Farmstead is a learning experience for the visitor. While James and Carol are "usually around," a call in advance can better ensure an open farm gate. The best time to go, however, is early to mid-July. The lavender is not only in full bloom with pick-your-own bouquet opportunities, but the Colorado Lavender Festival is in July, during which the Schotts dedicate themselves to educating tourists about their farm and the lavender. Carol leads the tour groups into the lavender field, sharing insight into Colorado's fledgling industry. Crouched near the buds, she describes different varieties and how to harvest the lavender, depending on the use. James demonstrates the lavender distillation process from which they derive the essential oils used in many of their products. He also puts his culinary training to the plate, preparing lavender infused offerings like olive tapenade (yes—lavender and olives!) served atop a bread round with Haystack goat cheese.

When the festival is over and the lavender is past it peak, the Schotts say they are the "ones out on the street at eleven at night trying to find our cows" or resting up for what unpredictability the next day brings. It's a lifestyle and location that aren't for everyone. Their visiting urbanite friends say it's beautiful, but…

James says, "We keep doing this because it feeds us." Figuratively and literally, Carol clarifies. "And that's something in a fine way we share with the people who were here long before we were," he says. "I like living in this house with its ghosts. I like being here because I know that there were other people who traipsed back and forth in this house before me. Particularly the people who built this and farmed here and had the orchard that's now gone."

"History provides a context," Carol adds. "It grounds you."

Meet Jeff Schwartz: Delicious Orchards and Big B's Fabulous Juices

Jeff Schwartz of Delicious Orchards and Big B's Fabulous Juices says it isn't only about local fare, about sustainability and good stewardship, about apples and cider. It's really about people—and their stories. The employees, neighbors, growers, vendors, consumers, friends and family are all one interconnected narrative to Jeff.

His story, the story of how he came to the North Fork Valley from New Jersey, begins in Russia. Jeff's agriculturist grandparents fled Odessa to escape the anti-Jewish pogroms in the early twentieth century. They settled in New Jersey within a community of dairy and chicken farmers, raising chickens themselves. His father was raised in the rural setting, but Jeff grew up in a typical Jersey suburbanite environment. He wondered what living on a farm would be like. Then, in his late teens, aiding a friend helped him determine his life's direction. "I distinctly remember rolling this wheelbarrow," he says.

"I was helping take care of this little greenhouse and I thought 'this is it, this is what I want to do.'"

He didn't jump right into overalls, however. First Jeff came to Boulder, Colorado, to go to college. There he got interested in the Navajos' relocation struggles at Big Mountain reservation in Arizona and decided to work down there. From them, he learned permaculture, an ecological-based agriculture practice that incorporates practices like water efficiency and soil erosion prevention. "For me," Jeff says, "that was the ultimate form of work: political activism and farming." Turns out, he wasn't the only one. He met his wife, Tracey, there while she was writing an article for *Earth Island Institute*.

They started a life together with a shared vision of sustainable farming, inspired in part by *The Good Life*, a philosophic account of an urban to rural experience written by Helen and Scott Nearing. After a few detours, they looked toward southwest Colorado in 1999. Jeff says a real estate agent in Ridgeway took one look at them—progressive, long hair—and said, "I think you should take a right at Delta and go up all the way to Paonia." They did, and when they got there, they knew, "This is exactly what we were looking for." In spite of the agent's assessment of the young couple, one of the reasons Paonia was an ideal community for them, Jeff notes, was because it wasn't a "super-progressive place with any one type of person." Artists and coal miners and bicycle cops all added to the diversity—as did Jeff and Tracey's jobs in order to make a living: beekeeping, peddling veggies roadside and custom tractor work. Fortunately, the latter brought Jeff to Big B's and Bernie Heideman.

Heideman started Big B's in the 1970s and was one of valley's first organic farmers. He ran the business out of a historic packing shed in Hotchkiss that had been home to area labels, including Grizzly. Jeff says that back then "all the apple growers from these mesas—Powell Mesa, Hanson Mesa—used to bring their apples to [this building]." They brought the fruit in bushel boxes, lowered it to the cellar through a trapdoor and brought it up to load onto the train when it was time to ship.

Jeff worked for Heideman for a couple years. He was making juice and labeling until, Jeff says, one day Bernie came to him with an offer: "Hey, Jeff. Would you like to buy this business? I'll carry the note, and I'll sell you the whole thing." Jeff and his brother Seth bought Big B's. Delicious Orchards followed some years later, where Jeff and his family now live so they can all be together, with everyone part of the daily story. He talks about how "in small communities the stories are so real, they're everyday. How do you not make a story out of harvesting 100,000 pounds of apples?" Jeff adds that his children see the stories take place in front of their eyes daily. "To them, it's very regular for me to pick them up in either this old dump truck full of apple pulp or in this Dodge loaded with 15,000 pounds of apples and then say, 'oh, I need an apple,' and then jumping and grabbing it…it's such a fabulous way for me to pass on stories and experience to them."

Resources

Print

Colorado Farm Fresh Directory
Colorado Department of Agriculture's free comprehensive guide to farmers' markets, roadside stands and wineries. It lists events and activities, as well as farm stay locations. The guide is available in print (check with the local chamber or tourism office) or online, with new mobile apps available for download.

Online

Chambers of Commerce
The chambers throughout the North Fork and Grand Valleys are community links to their fruit and wine country. Their websites' business, calendar and activity listings offer the person unfamiliar with the area an inside perspective. Northforkvalley.net is a unified effort of the valley's multiple chambers. Palisade.com is a direct branch to all things peaches and wine. Gjchamber. org is the Grand Valley's landing spot for a wide range of attractions.

Colorado.com
A wealth of resources at the tap of a keyboard: culinary activities, dinning and lodging, farm stays, tours, wines and wineries.

Colorado State University Extension
"High Altitude Food Preparation" (http://www.ext.colostate.edu/pubs/foodnut/p41.html). They also offer valuable food safety and canning resources online.

Grand Junction Sentinel

Their online publication features a calendar of events for the heritage and agritourist. Also included are links to stories—many by local expert and writer Dave Buchanan—and videos that provide additional topical insight.

orangepippin.com

A countrywide orchard guide that is "All about apples, pears, plums and cherries—and orchards where they are grown."

pickyourown.org

A guide to picking trips in northwest Colorado with canning/freezing resources.

Organizations

Colorado Farm Shares and CSAs

An online statewide list of community supported agriculture for those who wish to participate is available at coloradocsas.info.

Slow Food Western Slope

Member-based program promoting local producers, food and culture.

10

NIBBLES OF NOSTALGIA

The culinary bounty of Western Colorado has a history of its own. In the spirit of rural hospitality, fruit culture chefs—orchardists, enologists (and an entomologist), *fromagers* and historians—share a few of their recipes that have been inspired by their heritage and their harvests. Read. Eat. Drink. Enjoy!

FROM THE KITCHEN OF ANAMAE RICHMOND (AKA QUEEN OF THE APPLE BUTTER)

Anamae's family history is one of ranchers, miners and farmers—some of whom came to the Colorado Territory from the Idaho Territory in 1874. She is a chapter member of the Territorial Daughters of Colorado, an organization of "direct descendants" of settlers who were established by statehood in 1876. Their task is the preservation of this heritage and one that sometimes translates to the stovetop.

Apple Butter

This tasty tradition is made each fall on the antique wood cook stove at Cross Orchards Historic Site. Anamae prefers "Jonathan apples, as they produce

Cross Orchards volunteer Anamae Richmond makes apple butter each autumn on the antique stove in the bunkhouse. *Author photo.*

a beautiful red color in the finished product. Other apples such as Winesap and Rome Beauty can be used."

¼ bushel Jonathan apples
6–7 cups sugar
5 teaspoons cinnamon
1 teaspoon nutmeg
¼ teaspoon cloves

Wash apples and cut into quarters. Remove seedpods and stems as well as any blemishes. Do not peel. Place in large kettle and add about 2 inches of water. Boil until apples become very tender. Process through a food mill to make a thick pulp. Measure 16 cups of pulp in a large kettle and place on stove. Stir often while bringing to a boil and then add sugar, stirring to dissolve all sugar. Taste for sweetness; mixture should come to a good rolling boil. Adjust your heat and allow to thicken some. Add spices and stir in with a whisk to blend well. The spices can be adjusted to your liking—more or less. Can in hot sterilized mason jars and seal. It tastes wonderful on biscuits, toast, pancakes or cornbread.

Honey Fruit Cookies

"This is a recipe for cookies that were baked at Christmastime for as long as I can remember. My mother always made them, and her mother and grandmother made them. The fruit could be dried apples, peaches, cherries or apricots instead of raisins and coconut if they were available. My kids always helped me make them at Christmas, so they span several generations."

½ cup shortening
1 cup brown sugar
1 egg
½ cup honey
½ cup sour milk
1 teaspoon baking soda
2½ cups flour
1 teaspoon cinnamon
¼ teaspoon allspice

¼ teaspoon cloves
¼ cup raisins
¼ cup chopped nuts

Cream shortening and sugar and then add well-beaten egg, honey and milk. Sift dry ingredients into mixture, mix well and add fruit and nuts. Spread thin on greased baking pan. Bake 20 minutes at 350°F or until golden brown. Cool in pan, frost with thin glaze of frosting and cut into squares.

FROM THE KITCHEN OF BONNIE TALBOTT, MATRIARCH OF THE TALBOTT FAMILY FARMS CLAN

Packing Shed Cake

"This recipe came from Margaret Talbott [Harry Talbott's mother] who got it from an apple orchardist friend of hers."

Cake:
2 large eggs
1 cup olive oil
2 cups sugar
2 cups sifted flour
2 teaspoons cinnamon
1 teaspoon baking soda
½ teaspoon salt
1 teaspoon vanilla
4 cups thinly sliced apples
½–1 cup chopped nuts

Icing:
8 ounces cream cheese
3 tablespoons butter
1½ cups confectioner's sugar

Beat together eggs and oil until foamy. Add dry ingredients and vanilla. Batter will be very thick. Use hands to mix in apples and nuts. Place batter in greased 9- by 13-inch pan. Bake at 350°F for 45 minutes to 1 hour. When cake has cooled, mix cream cheese, butter and confectioner's sugar for icing. (Add more confectioner's sugar if needed.) Spread on cake. Makes 18–24 servings.

Pruner's Drink

"Pruning is mostly done in the winter—you can see the trees' shape best then. Pruners work as a team, in a group, and take breaks in the middle of the morning and afternoon. This warm drink became popular in the 1960s."

6 ounces Jell-O–any flavor
water

Dissolve Jell-O with 2 cups boiling water. Add 2 cups cool/warm water.

Freezer Peaches

"Freezer peaches are a staple for many uses such as peach shakes, ice cream, added to Jell-O, and [are] delicious stirred with cream while still frosty. Plastic 'freezer boxes' and ingredients set up in an assembly line fashion is a convenient way to fill the containers. Square, stackable containers work best for storage."

peaches
sugar
Fruit Fresh

Blanch peaches—scald for 1 to 3 minutes. Put in cold/ice water. Remove skin. Cut in half and pit.
    Set up four 1-pint freezer boxes (plastic freezer containers) in a row.
    For each box, set up ¼–½ cup sugar and 1 teaspoon Fruit Fresh. Place tomato slicer on top of the freezer box. Place half a peach, pit side down, on slicer and push through into freezer box. This is a

quick way to produce attractive, uniform slices. Fill each container halfway up with peaches. Sprinkle with half the sugar and half the Fruit Fresh. Add remaining peaches and top with remaining sugar and Fruit Fresh.

FROM THE KITCHEN OF GLENN FOSTER, OWNER/ WINEMAKER OF TALON WINE BRANDS: MEADERY OF THE ROCKIES, ST. KATHRYN CELLARS, TALON WINERY

Rhubarb Sauce with Yogurt

"This is one of my Dad's favorite breakfast items. Super simple and really delicious."

2 cups rhubarb
½ cup honey
¼ cup water

Chop fresh, clean rhubarb into 1-inch pieces. In saucepan, put ¼ cup of water and ½ cup of honey. Add the rhubarb, cover and cook over medium heat, stirring occasionally until rhubarb is completely softened and loose. Cool and refrigerate. Serve with plain, low-fat yogurt—about ⅓ of the total volume being sauce, ⅔ yogurt.

FROM THE KITCHEN OF PALISADE CHAMBER OF COMMERCE AND PEACH FESTIVAL CONTEST WINNER NASH HANNA

Peach Pizza

"The Peach Recipe Contest is almost twenty years old. This recipe is from one of our early winners." Nash Hanna took first prize for peach pizza in 1988.

Dough:

1 package active dry yeast
¼ cup warm water (110°F degrees)
⅓ cup margarine or butter, room temperature
¼ teaspoon salt
¼ cup sugar
1⅓ cups flour

Dissolve yeast in warm water, and let foam 5 minutes. Add butter, salt, sugar and about half of the flour. Mix, adding rest of flour until blended. Knead 5 minutes.

Filling:

6 ounces Philadelphia Cream Cheese
⅓ cup cottage cheese
⅓ cup powdered sugar
¼ teaspoon almond extract
¼ cup almonds
⅛ teaspoon nutmeg

Mix with mixer until blended.

Form dough into round circle, place on greased pizza pan. Spread cheese mixture on dough, bake at 350 degrees 15 to 20 minutes until brown.

Fruit:

8 peaches, pitted, peeled and sliced
1 tablespoon lemon juice

Combine in mixing bowl, cover.

Sauce:

1 cup peaches, peeled, pitted and sliced
1 cup water
1 tablespoon lemon juice
2½ tablespoons cornstarch
¼ teaspoon salt
¾ cup sugar

Smash peaches with potato masher in saucepan. Add water, lemon juice, cornstarch, salt and sugar. Cover over low heat for 10 to 15 minutes, cool 5 minutes and then arrange fruit mixture on pizza. Pour sauce over peaches. Refrigerate two hours. Decorate and serve.

FROM THE KITCHEN OF PALISADE INSECTARY MANAGER DAN BEAN (BY FAMILY MEMBERS ZEYNEP BEAN AND CANSEVER ÖZSOY)

"Lambsquarters (*Chenopodium album*) is a relative of spinach and is found in many gardens growing as a weed. It is widely known to be edible but few people take advantage of it. We have a really vigorous patch growing next to our vegetable garden so instead of trying to pull it out we decided to eat it; a biological control of sorts! My wife, Zeynep, makes lots of vegetable-rich Turkish dishes where lambsquarters can be added, especially as a spinach substitute.* She and my mother-in-law Cansever, who was here from Istanbul, wrote down some recipes. This one uses Colorado lamb and lambsquarters that our daughters gathered in our back yard. In Turkey, this dish is served on a bed of rice with yogurt on top, but it can be eaten just by itself also. *Afiyet olsun!*"

Lambsquarters with Colorado Ground Lamb

3 tablespoons olive oil

1 large onion, diced

1 pound ground lamb (we use Colorado lamb that we buy from a local rancher)

2 carrots, sliced thin

1 tomato, skin peeled, diced (or a can of diced tomatoes)

2 teaspoons pepper paste (or tomato paste)

½ cup rice, rinsed

1 pound lambsquarters, stems removed, washed

Optional: 2 tablespoons butter

Salt and pepper, to taste

Heat the olive oil in a large skillet and then cook the onion until tender. Add the ground lamb and brown, making sure to break the lumps with a spoon. Add salt to taste. Add the carrots, tomato, pepper paste and a little water to cover all, and let them cook until the carrots have softened. Add the rice, and stir the mixture. Now start putting in the lambsquarters in batches, stirring them in between each batch. As the leaves cook, they soften quite fast and leave room for more in the pot. After all of the lambsquarters are stirred in, pour some hot water (or broth) to cover the mixture, add the butter if you choose to, close the lid and simmer until the rice has cooked.

* Bean cautions: "If you decide to use lambsquarters, or any wild plant, as food, please make certain you know what you're harvesting."

From the Kitchen of Carol Schott of Lamborn Mountain Farmstead

Crostini with Truffle Oil, Lavender, Olive Oil and Herbed Goat Cheese

8 slices Italian bread or French baguette (½-inch thick)
½ cup olive paste (or finely chopped combination black and Kalamata olives)
1 teaspoon truffle oil
½ teaspoon ground culinary lavender
2 ounces soft white goat cheese mixed with ⅛ teaspoon Herbs de Provence olive oil

Preheat a skillet or griddle. Using a pastry brush, apply olive oil to both sides of bread slices. Fry bread until golden brown. Turn them and brown the other side. Finely chop olives in a food processor or chop fine on a cutting board.

In a small bowl, mix the olives, truffle oil and lavender together. Spread goat cheese mixture on each slice and top with olive mixture. Alternative if increasing portion: place slices on a cookie sheet and place in 400°F oven until golden.

Lavender Chevre Coffee Cake

½ cup butter

1½ cups "soft" chevre (If chevre is stiff, add small amount of sour cream or yogurt)

2 cups sugar

1 teaspoon ground lavender, optional (Use a coffee grinder or mortar and pestle)

2 eggs

1 teaspoon vanilla

2 cups flour

1 teaspoon baking powder

⅛ teaspoon salt

Filling:

¾ cup finely chopped nuts

4 tablespoons brown sugar

1½ tablespoons cinnamon

1 tablespoon culinary lavender buds

Cream butter, chevre and sugar (if using ground lavender, add to the butter mix).

Add eggs and vanilla.

Sift flour, baking powder and salt.

Gently mix flour mixture into batter until smooth.

Grease a Bundt cake pan or tube pan.

Place half of the batter in the pan, sprinkle filling over the batter, cover with the remaining batter and sprinkle lavender buds on top. Bake at 350°F for 90 minutes or until inserted knife is clean when removed. Let cool for 15 minutes before turning out.

FROM THE KITCHEN OF PALISADE'S CHILD AND MIGRANT SERVICES HEAD TAMALE CHEF, MARIA LOPEZ

Interpreted and reorganized for readability by Melissa Monahan Jankovsky. Find the original recipe handwritten in Spanish on A Bountiful History's Facebook page. Search: #MariaLopezEnchiladas.

Chicken Enchiladas with Green Chile Sauce
4 servings

1½ chicken breasts
1 white onion
2 tomatoes
1 bunch of green onion
5 tablespoons vegetable oil
12 corn tortillas
4 jalapeño chiles
1 can cream of chicken soup
1 [bunch] cilantro
1 clove garlic
¼ [pound] mozzarella cheese

Cook the chicken breasts in water, and when they are finished cooking, shred. Cut finely the white onion, tomato and green onion. Using part of the white onion, add it and tomato to the chicken and stew mixture. Put a little vegetable oil in a pan and heat. Lay the tortillas in oil until soft. Fill them with the chicken mixture and place in ovenproof dish. Blend in a blender the jalapeño chiles, cream of chicken, cilantro and garlic and pour over the rolled tortillas. Mix the rest of the white onion and cheese and sprinkle it on top and place in the oven for 30 minutes. Serve hot.

FROM THE KITCHEN OF THERESA HIGH OF HIGH COUNTRY ORCHARDS & VINEYARDS

"Serve with the remaining Colterris Coral White Cabernet Sauvignon or Colterris Cabernet Franc from Katie's Vineyard."

Fresh Peach Glazed Grilled Salmon

2 tablespoons butter
1 fillet of Copper River salmon (in season)

2 diced green onions
salt and pepper, to taste
2 fresh limes
2 cups Colterris Coral White Cabernet Sauvignon
¼ cup High Country Orchards Peach Preserve or Jalapeño Peach
Preserves
1 tree-ripened peach

Spread two tablespoons of butter on tin foil and place salmon fillet in foil. Sprinkle diced green onions over salmon. Salt and pepper to taste. Squeeze limes over the top. Place on grill and cup tin foil around the salmon fillet. Pour Colterris Coral wine over salmon. Close grill lid and grill for 20 minutes over medium-high heat. DO NOT OVERCOOK. Spoon ¼ cup of High Country Orchards Peach Preserve or Jalapeño Peach Preserves over the salmon fillet during the last 5 minutes of grilling. Remove while salmon is still moist. Garnish with fresh peach slices.

FROM THE KITCHEN OF CAROL ZADROZNY OF Z'S ORCHARD

"I have been making this Raw Apple Coffee Cake for fifty years. As a young bride, a wonderful neighbor shared this recipe with me. It is a no-fail easy-to-make real coffee cake because the liquid is coffee. This always-pleasing pleasure is shared at Z's Orchard every fall during apple harvest. I usually double this recipe and bake in large pan."

Raw Apple Coffee Cake

Cake:
1 cup sugar
1 egg
½ cup shortening
½ teaspoon baking soda
½ teaspoon cinnamon
½ teaspoon salt

½ cup warm coffee

2 cups chopped raw apples

Topping:

½ cup brown sugar

½ teaspoon cinnamon

½ cup chopped nuts

Mix cake ingredients in order given and pour into small baking dish.
Add toppings. Cover with foil and bake at 350°F for 30 minutes.

Part of FSA rural life documentation. Bringing peaches to the packing shed in Delta
County, taken in 1940. *Lee Russell photograph; courtesy Library of Congress.*

NOTES

CHAPTER 1

1. Alvin T. Steinel, *The History of Agriculture in Colorado* (Fort Collins, CO: State Agricultural College, 1926), 205.
2. Nolan J. Doesken, Roger A. Pielke Sr. and Odilia A.P. Bliss, "Climate of Colorado," http://ccc.atmos.colostate.edu/pdfs/climateofcoloradoNo.60.pdf.
3. Paul M. O'Rourke, *Frontier in Transition* (Denver, CO: Bureau of Land Management, 1980), 54.
4. Emma McCreanor, *Mesa County, Colorado* (Grand Junction: Museum of Western Colorado Press, 1986), 15.
5. Ernest Ingersoll, *Crest of the Continent* (Chicago: R.R. Donnelley & Sons, Lakeside Press, 1887), 297.
6. Land Trust Alliance, "Colorado, Palisade Fruitlands—FRPP Economic Research," 2012, http://www.landtrustalliance.org/policy/documents/colorado-frpp-report.
7. Steinel, *History of Agriculture*, 507–08
8. Mary Rait, "Development of Grand Junction and the Colorado River Valley to Palisade from 1881 to 1931—Part I," *Journal of the Western Slope* 3, no. 3 (1988).
9. Steinel, *History of Agriculture*, 505.
10. Ibid.
11. Ibid., 508–09
12. Duane Vandenbusche and Duane A. Smith. *A Land Alone* (Boulder, CO: Pruett Publishing Company, 1981), 149.

13. O'Rourke, *Frontier in Transition*, 130.

14. National Archives, "Our Documents—Homestead Act (1862)," http://www.ourdocuments.gov/doc.php?flash=true&doc=31.

15. Steven F. Mehls, "Valley of Opportunity: History of West-Central Colorado," *Cultural Resources Series* 12 (Denver, CO: Bureau of Land Managment, 1982), 131.

16. Ibid., 161.

17. Ibid., 139.

18. Denver and Rio Grande Railroad, "The Fertile Lands of Colorado and Northern New Mexico," Library of Congress. https://archive.org/details/fertilelandsofc00denv.

19. Dennis Clark, author interview, September 24, 2014.

20. Rait, "Development of Grand Junction."

21. Mehls, "Valley of Opportunity," 131–32.

22. McCreanor, *Mesa County*, 14.

23. *Annual Report of the State Board of Horticulture*, ed. Martha A. Shute (Colorado Department of Education, 1911), http://www2.cde.state.co.us/artemis/agserials/ag116internet/ag1161910internet.pdf.

24. McCreanor, *Mesa County*, 15.

25. Ibid., 14.

26. Steinel, *History of Agriculture*, 512.

27. E.H. Siegler and H.K. Plank, *Life History of the Codling Moth in the Grand Valley of Colorado* (Washington, D.C.: U.S. Department of Agriculture, n.d.), https://archive.org/stream/lifehistoryofcod932sieg/lifehistoryofcod932sieg_djvu.txt.

28. Carrie Clark, "The Bug House," *Journal of the Western Slope* 14, no. 3 (1999): 4.

29. McCreanor, *Mesa County*, 14.

30. O'Rourke, *Frontier in Transition*, 103, 129.

31. Dennis Clark, interview.

32. O'Rourke, *Frontier in Transition*, 156.

33. Mehls, "Valley of Opportunity," 243, 253.

34. McCreanor, *Mesa County*, 15.

35. Steve Ela, author interview, September 8, 2014.

36. *Souvenir of the North Fork Valley Colorado*, (Paonia: The Newspaper, 1905).

37. "Hotchkiss: The Main Event," *North Fork Times*, 1909 (newsprint copy from Hotchkiss Crawford Museum).

38. Paonia, Hotchkiss and Crawford Chambers of Commerce.

39. Vandenbusche and Smith, *A Land Alone*, 211.

40. O'Rourke, *Frontier in Transition*, 131.

41. Ibid., 156.

42. Barbara Bowman, "The Peach Festival, 1887–1909: A Celebration of the Land," *Journal of the Western Slope* (1987): 22–33.

43. William L. McGuire and Charles Teed, *The Fruit Belt Route* (Grand Junction, CO: National Railway Historical Society, 1981), 33.

44. Colorado Department of Agriculture, Plant Industry Division, http://www.sos.state.co.us/CCR/GenerateRulePdf.do?ruleVersionId=486.

CHAPTER 2

45. *Annual Report of the State Board of Horticulture*, 1911, 43.

46. The Global Wine Industry, "Wine Culture in Europe," https://web.duke.edu/soc142/team5/europeanmarket.html.

47. Teresa Sales, "Terror Creek Winery Recreates Fromer Paonia Showcase," *Delta County Imperial*, September 1993.

48. McCreanor, *Mesa County*, 15.

49. Michael Moloney, "A History of the Palisade Wine Industry," *Journal of the Western Slope* 11, no. 2 (1996): 1–21.

50. Doug Caskey, "Colorado Wine: Rooted in History," http://coloradowine.com/cms/index.cfm/feature/238_41/colorado-wine-rooted-in-history.cfm.

51. Steinel, *History of Agriculture*, 505.

52. "History: A Chronology of Events," Colorado Wine, http://www.coloradowine.com.

53. John R. McKivigan, "A Brief History of the American Abolitionist Movement," http://americanabolitionist.liberalarts.iupui.edu/brief.htm.

54. Ken Burns and Lynn Novick, *Prohibition: Roots of Prohibition* (PBS, 2011), http://www.pbs.org/kenburns/prohibition/roots-of-prohibition/.

55. Abbott Fay, *The Story Of Colorado Wines* (Montrose, CO: Western Reflections Publishing Company, 2002), 5.

56. Deets Picket, Clarence True Wilson and Ernest Dailey Smith, *The Cyclopedia of Temperance, Prohibition and Public Morals* (New York/Cincinnati: Methodist Book Concern, 1917), 351, http://darrow.law.umn.edu/documents/The_Cyclopedia_of_Temperance_Prohibition_1917.pdf.

57. *Los Angeles Herald*, March 26, 1907, California Digital Newspaper Collection, http://cdnc.ucr.edu/cgi-bin/cdnc?a=d&d=LAH19070326.2.34.

58. Frank Gibbard, "'Medicinal' Alcohol and Colorado's Local Option Law," *Colorado Lawyer* 43, no. 6 (June 2014), http://www.cobar.org/tcl/tcl_articles.cfm?articleid=8557.

59. Fay, *Story of Colorado Wines*, 5.

60. Dennis Polhill, "Initative and Referendum in Colorado," University of Southern California, 2006, http://www.iandrinstitute.org/REPORT%202006-4%20Colorado.pdf.

61. Mehls, "Valley of Opportunity," 168.

62. Sharon Sullivan, "A Toast to the Ivancies," *Post Independent*, September 13, 2007, http://www.postindependent.com/article/20070914/COMMUNITY_NEWS/70913014 (accessed December 28, 2014).

63. Moloney, "Palisade Wine Industry," 2.

64. Ibid., 3.

65. Ibid.

66. Ibid., 5.

67. Rick Turley, author interview, August 29, 2014.

68. Moloney, "Palisade Wine Industry," 8.

69. Eugene A. Mielke, *Grape and Wine Production in the Four Corners Region* (University of Arizona Agricultural Experiment Station, Technical Bulletin 239, 1980), Introduction.

70. State of Colorado. "12-47-103. Definitions. (15)," (Colorado 61st General Assembly, 1997), http://tornado.state.co.us/gov_dir/leg_dir/olls/sl1997/sl_80.htm.

71. United States Securities and Exchange Commission, "Willamette Valley Vineyards, Inc. 12/31/2011 10-K," http://www.sec.gov/Archives/edgar/data/838875/000119983512000142/willamette_12312011-10k.htm.

72. State of Colorado, "12-47-106. Exemptions. (5)," (*Colorado 66th General Assembly, 2008*) http://tornado.state.co.us/gov_dir/leg_dir/olls/sl2008a/sl_420.htm.

73. "Overview and Background of the CO Wine Board's funding of research performed by Colorado State University and a perspective on the Ram's Point Winery for research and instruction," (CWIDB, 2012), http://www.coloradowine.com/cms/index.cfm/feature/211_48/csu-rams-point-winery-and-background.cfm.

74. Glenn Foster, author interview, October 8, 2014.

75. Colorado Wine Industry Development Board (CWIDB), "Canyon Wind Cellars Wins Best of Show in Annual Colorado Wine Competition," http://www.coloradowine.com/cms/index.cfm/feature/302_22/canyon-wind-takes-2014-governors-cup.cfm.

76. Jay Christianson, author interview, November 3, 2014.

77. CWIDB, "Canyon Wind Cellars."

78. Cassidee Shull, author interview, August 29, 2014.

Chapter 3

79. Land Trust Alliance, "Colorado, Palisade Fruitlands—FRPP Economic Research," 2012, http://www.landtrustalliance.org/policy/documents/colorado-frpp-report.

80. Harold Zimmerman, "Harvesting Peaches with German Prisoners of War," *Journal of the Western Slope* 2, no. 1 (1987): 18–21.
81. Land Trust Alliance, "Palisade Fruitlands."
82. Mehls, "Valley of Opportunity," 146–47.
83. Davie Munoz, *Hands That Harvest* (Grand Junction, CO: Farolito Press, 2004), 7.
84. Ibid., 8.
85. Mehls, "Valley of Opportunity," 140–41.
86. Priscilla Walker, author interview, August 25, 2014.
87. Munoz, *Hands That Harvest*, 9–10.
88. Rait, "Development of Grand Junction," 48.
89. Mehls, "Valley of Opportunity," 216, 219.
90. Munoz, *Hands That Harvest*, 11.
91. O'Rouke, *Frontier in Transition*, 156.
92. Kristi Mease, "The Labor Shortage and Its Solution During WWII in the Grand Valley of Western Colorado," *Journal of the Western Slope* 7, no. 3 (1992), 1–5.
93. Zimmerman, "Harvesting Peaches."
94. Dennis Clark, interview.
95. Mease, "Labor Shortage," 2.
96. Munoz, *Hands That Harvest*, 13.
97. University of Northern Colorado, "The Bracero Program," http://www.unco.edu/cohmlp/pdfs/Bracero_Program_PowerPoint.pdf.
98. Munoz, *Hands That Harvest*, 18, 84.
99. Munoz, *Hands That Harvest*, 15, 16, 21.
100. Ibid., 16, 18, 20, 21, 85.
101. Karalyn Dorn, author interview, October 22, 2014.
102. Land Trust Alliance, "Palisade Fruitlands."

CHAPTER 4

103. Donald A. MacKendrick, "The Roan Creek Toll Road," *Journal of the Western Slope* 2, no. 1 (1987): 2–3.
104. Paul H. Bardell Jr., *Peaches and Politics in Palisade, Colorado* (West Conshohocken, PA: Infinity Publishing, 2009), 14.
105. O'Rouke, *Frontier in Transition*, 94.
106. Rait, "Development of Grand Junction," 24.
107. Mehls, "Valley of Opportunity," 87.
108. Vandenbusche and Smith, *A Land Alone*, 149.
109. McGuire and Teed, *Fruit Belt Route*, 27, 49–50.
110. Willaim L. Reich, *Colorado Railroad Ice Houses* (Golden: Colorado Railroad Museum, 2010).

111. Pamela Bouton, "Solid Cold," *Journal of the Western Slope* 5, no. 4 (1990), 40.

112. Ibid., 12, 30, 40–41, 44.

113. Rait, "Development of Grand Junction," 33.

114. Marilyn Bruce Tate, author interview, September 10, 2014.

115. Rait, "Development of Grand Junction," 39.

116. Mehls, "Valley of Opportunity," 141.

117. *Souvenir of the North Fork Valley, Colorado.*

118. Rait, "Development of Grand Junction," 44.

119. Walker, interview.

120. Harry Talbott, author interview, August 29, 2014.

CHAPTER 5

121. Norris Hundley Jr., *Water and the West*, 2nd ed. (Berkley: University of California Press, 2009), 17.

122. Darryll Olsen, "The Economic Importance of Western Irrigated Agriculture," Environmental Protection Agency, 2012, http://water.epa. gov/action/importanceofwater/upload/12-Olsen.pdf.

123. U.S. Geological Survey, "River Basins of the United States: Colorado," 1987, http://pubs.usgs.gov/gip/70039371/report.pdf.

124. Ibid.

125. Abbott Fay, "Mountain Men/Trappers," Grand County History, http:// stories.grandcountyhistory.org/category/mountain-men-trappers.

126. Mehls, "Valley of Opportunity," 202.

127. U.S. Congress, Renaming of the Grand River, Colorado. Hearing before the Committee on Interstate and Foreign Commerce of the House of Representatives on H.J. Res. 460. 66th Cong., 3rd sess. Washington, D.C.: GPO, 1921, Colorado State Libraries, Digital Collections, http://digitool. library.colostate.edu/R/?func=dbin-jump-full&object_id=80825.

128. Steinel, *History of Agriculture*, 244.

129. Jerry Spangler, "Tracking the Anasazi," *Surveyor* 12, no. 4 (2014): 11, www. coloradoarchaeology.org/PUBLICATIONS/Newsletters/TheSurveyor-2014Fall.pdf.

130. Susan Eininger et al., "Archaeological Resources in Southwestern Colorado," Bureau of Land Management, 1982, 42, 164, http:// www.blm.gov/style/medialib/blm/wo/Planning_and_Renewable_ Resources/coop_agencies/new_documents/co3.Par.66322.File.dat/ NickensArchaeological.pdf.

131. Eininger et al., "Archaeological Resources," 74, 80.

132. Steinel, *History of Agriculture*, 170.

133. Western Regional Climate Center, "Climate of Colorado," http://www.wrcc.dri.edu/narratives/COLORADO.htm.

134. Mehls, "Valley of Opportunity," 27, 195.

135. "What's in Store," Colorado Water Conservation Board, Legislative Lunch, 2010, http://cwcb.state.co.us/water-management/water-supply-planning/Documents/LegislativeUpdateCOWaterSupplyFuture.pdf.

136. "Prior Appropriation Law," Colorado Division of Water Resources, http://water.state.co.us/surfacewater/swrights/pages/priorapprop.aspx.

137. William E. Pabor, *Colorado as an Agricultural State* (New York: Orange Judd Company, 1883), 37.

138. Steinel, *History of Agriculture*, 235.

139. Flora Cooper Locke, "Recollections of Naturita," *Journal of the Western Slope* 1, no. 4 (1986): 36.

140. Steinel, *History of Agriculture*, 190.

141. Don Davidson, "The Grand River Ditch," *Journal of the Western Slope* 1, no. 4 (1986): 1–30.

142. Max Schmidt, author interview, October 6, 2004.

143. Schmidt, interview.

144. Center for Columbia River History, "Reclaimation Act/Newlands Act of 1902," http://www.ccrh.org/comm/umatilla/primary/newlands.htm.

145. Theodore Roosevelt, "TR Center—Message of the President of the United States Comm," Roosevelt Center, 1902, http://www.theodorerooseveltcenter.org/Research/Digital-Library/Record.aspx?libID=o284538.

146. National Park Service, "Capitol Reef NP," Chapter 3, http://www.nps.gov/parkhistory/online_books/care/adhi/adhi3.htm National Park Service.

147. Bureau of Land Management, "Grand Valley Project," 1994, 17, http://www.usbr.gov/projects/ImageServer?imgName=Doc_1305042485344.pdf.

148. Colorado Watershed Assembly, "Colorado Water Facts," 2015, http://www.coloradowater.org/Colorado%20Water%20Facts.

149. Colorado Basin Roundtable, "Providing for Colorado's Statewide and West Slope Water Needs," 2013, http://cwcbweblink.state.co.us/WebLink/ElectronicFile.aspx?docid=173880&&dbid=0.

150. Ibid.

CHAPTER 6

151. Brian Collier, "Teach the Starlings," http://teachstarlings.societyrne.net/html/intro.htm.

152. National Wildlife Research Center, "European Starlings: A Review of an Invasive Species with Far-Reaching Impacts," 2007, 378, http://

www.aphis.usda.gov/wildlife_damage/nwrc/publications/07pubs/linz076.pdf.

153. *Annual Report of the State Board of Horticulture*, vol. 10 (State of Colorado Board of Horticulture, 1899), 48, http://www2.cde.state.co.us/artemis/agserials/ag116internet/ag1161898internet.pdf.

154. Ibid., 26.

155. Siegler and Plank, "Life History."

156. *Annual Report of the State Board of Horticulture*, vol. 10, 8.

157. *Annual Report of the State Board of Horticulture*, 1911, 111. http://www2.cde.state.co.us/artemis/agserials/ag116internet/ag1161910internet.pdf.

158. Clark, "Bug House," 2–3.

159. Colorado Department of Agriculture, "Organic," 2013, https://www.colorado.gov/agmarkets/organic-0.

160. Clark, "Bug House," 6.

161. Ibid., 8, 11.

162. Department of Agriculture, Plant Industry Division.

163. Vincyclopedia, "Plylloxera," Professional Friends of Wine, 2012, http://www.winepros.org/wine101/vincyc-phylloxera.htm.

164. Ela, interview.

165. Richard A. Hamman Jr., Steven D. Savage and Harold J. Larsen, *The Colorado Grape Growers' Guide* (Ft. Collins: Colorado State Universty, 1998), 49.

166. Guy Ames, "Peaches," National Sustainable Agriculture Information Service, 2012, 19, http://www.agrihortico.com/freedownloads/peaches.pdf.

167. Dawn Thilmany, "The US Organic Industry," Colorado State University, 2006, 2, http://organic.colostate.edu/documents/Thilmany_paper.pdf.

168. United States Department of Agriculture, "Organic Agriculture," 2012, table 42, http://www.agcensus.usda.gov/Publications/2012/Full_Report/Volume_1,_Chapter_2_County_Level/Colorado/st08_2_042_042.pdf.

169. Timothy J. Larsen and Summer Jones, "Colorado's Expanding Organic Industry," Markets Division, Colorado Department of Agriculture, https://www.colorado.gov/pacific/sites/default/files/Colorados%20Expanding%20Organic%20Industry_0.pdf.

170. Colorado Department of Agriculture, "Organic."

171. James H. Baker, "History of Colorado," Colorado State Historical Society, 1927, 637–38, https://archive.org/stream/historycolorad02stat/historycolorad02stat_djvu.txt.

172. Ibid., 639.

173. D.W. Working, *Something About the Bee Industry in Colorado*, National Bee-Keepers' Association, 1902, http://archive.org/stream/cu31924003245259/cu31924003245259_djvu.txt%201902%20report:.

174. Ibid.

175. Vandenbusche and Smith, *A Land Alone*, 152.

176. A. Gaus and H. Larsen, "Pollination of Tree Fruits," Colorado State University Extension, 2009, http://www.ext.colostate.edu/pubs/garden/07002.html.

177. Nancy Lofholm, "Africanized Bees Reach Colorado," *Denver Post*, 2014, http://www.denverpost.com/news/ci_25754005/africanized-bees-reach-colorado-turn-up-palisade-orchard.

178. Universiteit Utrecht, "Present Scale of Use of Neonicotinoids Put Pollinator Service at Risk," 2013, http://pers.uu.nl/scientists-urge-transition-to-pollinator-friendly-agriculture.

179. Diana Gitig, "More Problems for Bees," Ars Technica, 2014, http://arstechnica.com/science/2014/11/more-problems-for-bees-weve-wiped-out-their-favorite-plants/#p3.

180. Western Sustainable Agriculture Research and Education Program, "Colorado Queen Honey Bee Testing Project," 2015, https://coloradoqueenhoneybeetestingproject.wordpress.com/about/.

CHAPTER 7

181. W.C. McKern, "Western Colorado Petroglyphs," Bureau of Land Management, 1983, http://www.blm.gov/pgdata/etc/medialib/blm/wo/Planning_and_Renewable_Resources/coop_agencies/new_documents/co3.Par.28150.File.dat/mckern.pdf.

182. U.S. National Park Service, "Quilt Discovery Experience," 2015, http://www.nps.gov/home/planyourvisit/quilt-discovery-experience.htm."

183. Quilting in America, "History of Quilts in American Folkart," 2009, http://www.quilting-in-america.com/History-of-Quilts.html.

184. Verda, author interview, February 24, 2015.

185. Tate, interview.

186. Theresa High, author interview, November 21, 2014.

187. Colorado Creative Industries, "Communities/Creative District Certification," 2015, http://www.coloradocreativeindustries.org/communities/creative-district-certification.

188. Kay Crane, author interview, October 8, 2014.

189. Kay Fiegel, author interview, October 9, 2014.

CHAPTER 8

190. North Fork Heart & Soul Project, "What Matters Most to the Future of the North Fork Valley," 2014, 13–15. http://www.northforkheartsoul.com/.

191. Dennis Clark, interview.

192. Ela, interview.

193. Harry Talbott, interview.

194. Charlie Talbott, author interview, August 29, 2014.

195. American AgCredit, "Generations: The Talbott Family," 2014, 2 min., 27 sec., http://youtu.be/NSfB1OEBwo4.

196. Land Trust Alliance, "Palisade Fruitlands," 9.

197. Mesa Land Trust, "Lands for Tomorrow," 2014, 1, http://mesalandtrust. org/wp-content/uploads/MLT-014-Annual-Report.pdf.

198. Mesa Land Trust, "Lands for Tomorrow," 3.

199. National Young Farmers Coalition, http://www.youngfarmers.org/ about/our-work/.

200. Colorado Department of Agriculture, "Wine, Beer & Spirits," 2015, https://www.colorado.gov/pacific/agmarkets/wine-beer-spirits.

201. Colorado Brewers Guild, "Craft Brewers Industry Overview and Economic Impact 2012 and 2013," 2014, 1, http://coloradobeer.org/ wp-content/uploads/2011/03/White-Paper_Colorado-Brewers-Guild-Economic-Impact-Study_Final-Report-2014.pdf.

202. Tom Wilmes, "Better When Wet," *Draft*, 2012, http://draftmag.com/ wet-fresh-hop-beer/.

203. Rob Masters, "Rise of the Colorado Distilling Scene," *Colorado Business Review* 78 no. 12 (2012), 3–5.

204. Kids' Pasta Project, http://www.kidspastaproject.org/.

205. Young Americans Center for Financial Education, "Competition Results: 2009 Celebration for Young Entrepreneurs Winners and Finalists," http://registration.yacenter.org/index.cfm?fuseAction=celebr ationForYoungEntrepreneurs.CompetitionResults.

206. Cassandra Shenk, author interview, February 25, 2014.

INDEX

ABOUT THE AUTHOR

J odi Buchan is a writer always in pursuit of a good story. Her essays, articles and poems have been featured in regional, national and online publications, including the *Aspen Sojourner* and *Northwoods Woman Magazine*, as well as *The Bark* and *Exceptional Parent*. While working at a marketing agency, she wrote blogs and other social media content for clients to help them tell their Internet narratives.

Buchan's own blogs are A Bountiful Heritage, which is about food, wine and farm culture, and DD Awareness, a site dedicated to caregivers of people with developmental disabilities—people like her daughter, Katie.

Carbondale, Colorado, near Aspen is now home for this native North Dakotan, but she still keeps a jar of North Dakota black dirt on the desk to honor her roots, her pioneering ancestors and where food really comes from.

A BOUNTIFUL HERITAGE

Enterprising pioneers transformed the isolated lands of the North Fork and Grand Valleys into blossoming oases. Sowing cultural roots in this arid rocky landscape, the settlers cultivated what became delectable destinations boasting world-class wine and award-winning fruit. Midwestern immigrants cultivated orchards, Europeans produced their own table wine and growers delivered their harvest by horse and wagon to the first locavore market—area miners. Sit down, pour a glass of wine or cider and join journalist Jodi Buchan on a journey through the Western Slope's fruit and wine country. Meet orchardists and viticulturists, and celebrate the discoveries, traditions and innovations thriving today across the region.

AMERICAN PALATE